Labor and Freedom

Eugene V. Debs

MISCELLANY

THE OLD UMBRELLA MENDER. Coming Nation, March 1, 1913.

It was on a cold morning late in November last, just after the national election, and I was walking briskly toward my office. A stiff wind was blowing and a drizzling rain was falling. The threads in one of the ribs of my umbrella snapped asunder and the cover flew upward, as it has a way of doing, and I was about to lower my disabled shower-stick when I ran slapdash into an old itinerant umbrella mender with his outfit slung across his back and shuffling along in the opposite direction. He had noticed the ill-behavior of my umbrella. It snapped from its bearing even as he had his eyes upon it. Perhaps it understood. Anyway he had not a cent in his pocket and he had not yet breakfasted that cold and wet November morning.

He was about 65. His clothes had evidently weathered many a storm and besides being worn and shabby were too light for that season. Overcoat he had none. Nor gloves, nor overshoes. Mine embarrassed me.

His hat had been brushed to a standstill. His shoes were making their last stand and a protruding toe, red with the cold, seemed to have been shoved out as a signal of distress.

The outfit of the old fellow, carried on his back, was sorry enough to fit his general makeup, and if he had offered himself for sale just as he stood, including his earthly belongings and his immortal soul, he would have found no bidder nor brought a cent.

The face of the old umbrella mender lighted up with a kindly smile as he commented on the strange conduct of my umbrella in slipping a cog just as he happened to come along. I asked him by what evil magic he did the trick and he laughed in a half-hearted way just to be polite, but it was plain

3

that he had long since forgotten how to laugh.

As we stepped into the shelter of an adjoining store he sat down on the steps and drawing a threaded needle from beneath the lapel of his thin and faded coat, he began to sew the cover back into its proper place. His fingers were red and numb. A discolored nail partly hid a badly bruised thumb.

He had difficulty in doing this bit of sewing, and it plainly distressed him. His eyesight was failing and his fingers were stiff in the joints. Yet he strove eagerly and intently to master their dumb protest. And he hoped, as he remarked, that he would be able to make an extra bit of money to provide himself with a pair of spectacles, now that favorable weather had set in for his trade.

Poor human soul, I thought to myself, as I looked down upon the weatherbeaten brother at my feet! A vagabond dog among his kind would fare better than this worn-out old umbrella mender in a civilized human community.

The warm clothes I had on made me uncomfortable as I saw him sitting there in rags mending my umbrella. The overcoat I wore made me ashamed of myself. Every time the umbrella mender looked up out of his rags I winced.

What crime had he committed that condemned him to go through the world in tatters to be lashed by the merciless blasts of winter and tormented by hunger-pangs, and of what rare virtue was I possessed that entitled me to wear the best of clothes and eat the choicest food!

Dared I call him brother? And could I call him brother without insulting him?

These were the reflections that agitated my mind and troubled my heart.

"Good morning!" was the cheery greeting of a man who passed on the sidewalk, calling me by name.

The old umbrella mender fairly started at the mention of my name. He had just completed his bit of sewing and the threaded needle fell from his fingers.

"Excuse me!" he said timidly, "is this Mr. Debs?"

"Yes," I answered.

4

"Eugene V. Debs?"

"Yes, brother."

"Thank God," exclaimed the old umbrella mender as he fairly bounded to his feet and seized my extended hand with both of his. There were tears in his eyes and his face was flushed.

"Of course I know you now," he went on. "This is your home and I have often seen your picture. But this is the first time I have ever seen you and if it hadn't been for your umbrella snapping just as I came along, I would have passed you by and the chances are that I never would have seen you. God must have tipped off your umbrella to give me a stop-signal."

"Say, Gene," he continued, still holding me with both hands, "I am pretty well down, ain't I? About all in and making my last stand before shuffling off."

"But say, Gene, I never scabbed. Look at these hands! I'm an old rail and I followed the business for twenty-seven years. I broke and ran a freight train most of that time. Never got a passenger run because I was too active on grievance committees and called a firebrand by the officials. I wouldn't stand for any of their dirty work. If I'd been like some of 'em I'd had a passenger train years ago and been saved lots of grief. But I'd rather be a broken down old umbrella-fixer without a friend than to be a scab and worth a million."

A gleam of triumph lighted up his seamed and weatherbeaten countenance.

"Did you belong to the A. R. U.?" I asked.

"Did I?" he answered with peculiar and assuring emphasis. "I was the first man on our division to sign the list, and my name was first on the charter. Look it up and you'll find me there. My card I lost in Ohio where I was run in as a vag. The deputy that searched me at the jail took my card from my pocket and I never saw it again. It was all I had left. I raised a row about it and they threatened to lock me up again. I was told afterwards that the deputy had scabbed in the A. R. U. strike."

"Did I belong to the A. R. U.? Well, I should say I did and I am proud of it even if they did put me on the hummer and pull me down to where I am today. But I never scabbed. And when I cross the big divide I can walk straight up to the bar of judgment and look God in the face without a

5

flicker."

"We had the railroads whipped to a standstill," he said, warming up, "but the soldiers, the courts and the army of deputy United States marshals that scabbed our jobs were too much for us. It was the government and not the railroads that put us out, and it was a sorry day for the railroad men of this country. Mark what I tell you, the time will come when they will have to reorganize the A. R. U. It was the only union that all could join and in which all got a square deal, and it was the only union the railroad managers ever feared."

And then he told me the melancholy story of his own persecution and suffering after the strike. His job was gone and his name was on the blacklist. Five jobs he secured under assumed names were lost to him as soon as he was found out. Poverty began to harass him. He picked up odd jobs and when he managed to get a dollar ahead he sent it to his family. His aged mother died of privation and worry and his wife soon followed her to the grave. Two boys were left, but whatever became of them and whether they are now alive or dead, he could never learn.

The old fellow grew serious and a melancholy sigh escaped him. But he was not bitter. He bore no malice toward any one. He had suffered much, but he had kept the faith, and his regrets were at least free from reproach.

He was a broken down old veteran of the industrial army. He had paid the penalties of his protest against privately owned industry and the slavery of his class, and now in his old age he was shuffling along in his rags toward a nameless grave in the pottersfield.

Had he been an obedient corporation lackey; had he scabbed on his fellow-workers; had he been mean and selfish and cold-blooded, he would have been promoted instead of blacklisted by the corporation and honored instead of hounded by society. His manhood and self-respect cost him dearly, but he paid the price to the last farthing. His right to work and live, his home, his family and his friends were all swept away because he refused to scab on his fellowmen.

The old umbrella mender stood before me proud and erect and looked me straight in the eyes as he finished his pathetic story.

The shabby clothes he wore were to him capitalist society's reward of manhood and badge of honor.

There was something peculiarly grand about the scarred old veteran of the industrial battlefield. His shabbiness was all on the outside, and he seemed transfigured to me and clad in garments of glory. He loomed before me like a forest-monarch the tempests had riven and denuded of its foliage but could not lay low.

He had kept the faith and had never scabbed!

dec

THE SECRET OF EFFICIENT EXPRESSION. Coming Nation, July 8, 1911.

The following was written for the Department of Education of the University of Wisconsin, under whose direction there is being conducted an investigation of the subject of "Distinguished Contemporary Orators or Lecturers—With special reference to fertility and efficiency of expression. What is the key to their ability as masters of language? What school subjects, or what kinds of training have entered into their lives that have given them power to express themselves effectively?"

The secret of efficient expression in oratory—if secret it can properly be called—is in having something efficient to express and being so filled with it that it expresses itself. The choice of words is not important since efficient expression, the result of efficient thinking, chooses its own words, moulds and fashions its own sentences, and creates a diction suited to its own purposes.

In my own case the power of expression is not due to education or to training. I had no time for either and have often felt the lack of both. The schools I attended were primitive and when I left them at fourteen to go to work I could hardly write a grammatical sentence; and to be frank I am not quite sure that I can do so now. But I had a retentive memory and was fond of committing and declaiming such orations and poems as appealed to me. Patrick Henry's revolutionary speech had first place. Robert Emmet's immortal oration was a great favorite and moved me deeply. Drake's "American Flag" stirred my blood as did also Schiller's "Burgschaft." Often I felt myself thrilled under the spell of these, recited to myself, inaudibly at times, and at others declaimed boldly and dramatically, when no one else was listening.

Everything that was revolutionary appealed to me and it was this that made Patrick Henry one of my first heroes; and my passion for his eloquent and burning defiance of King George inspired the first speech I ever attempted in public, with Patrick himself as the theme. This was before the Occidental Literary Club of Terre Haute, Ind., of which I was then a member, and I still shudder as I recall the crowded little club-room which greeted me, and feel again the big drops of cold sweat standing out all over me as I realized the plight I was in and the utter hopelessness of escape.

The spectacle I made of myself that evening will never be effaced from my memory, and the sympathetic assurances of my friends at the close of the exhibition did not relieve the keen sense of humiliation and shame I felt for the disgrace I had brought upon myself and my patron saint. The speech could not possibly have been worse and my mortification was complete. In my heart I hoped most earnestly that my hero's spiritual ears were not attuned to the affairs of this earth, at least that evening.

It was then I realized and sorely felt the need of the education and training I had missed and then and there I resolved to make up for it as best I could. I set to work in earnest to learn what I so much needed to know. While firing a switch-engine at night I attended a private school half a day each day, sleeping in the morning and attending school in the afternoon. I bought an encyclopedia on the installment plan, one volume each month, and began to read and study history and literature and to devote myself to grammar and composition.

The revolutionary history of the United States and France stirred me deeply and its heroes and martyrs became my idols. Thomas Paine towered above them all. A thousand times since then I have found inspiration and strength in the thrilling words, "These are the times that try men's souls."

Here I should say, for the purpose of this writing, that from the time I began to read with a serious mind, feeling keenly as I did my lack of knowledge, especially the power of proper expression, both oral and written, I observed the structure and studied the composition of every paragraph and every sentence, and when one appeared striking to me, owing to its perfection of style or phrasing, I read it a second time or perhaps committed it to memory, and this became a fixed habit which I retain to this day, and if I have any unusual command of language it is because I have made it a life-long practice to cultivate the art of expression in a sub-conscious study of the structure and phrasing of every paragraph in my readings.

It was while serving an apprenticeship in a railroad shop and in later years as a locomotive fireman and as a wage worker in other capacities that I came to realize the oppressions and sufferings of the working class and to understand something of the labor question. The wrongs existing here I knew from having experienced them, and the irresistible appeal of these wrongs to be righted determined my destiny. I joined a labor union and from that time to this the high ambition, the controlling purpose of my life has been the education, organization and emancipation of the working class. It was this passionate sympathy with my class that gave me all the power I have to serve it. I felt their suffering because I was one of them and I began to speak and write for them for the same reason. In this there was no altruism, no self-sacrifice, only duty. I could not have done otherwise. Had I attempted it I should have failed. Such as I have been and am, I had to be.

I abhorred slavery in every form. I yearned to see all men and all women free. I detested the idea of some men being ruled by others, and of women being ruled by men. I believed that women should have all the rights men have, and I looked upon child labor as a crime. And so I became an agitator and this ruling passion of my life found larger expression.

In the clash of conflict which followed and the trials incident to it I grew stronger. The notoriety which came in consequence enlarged my hearing with the people and this in turn demanded more efficient means of expression. The cause that was sacred to me was assailed. My very life and honor were on trial. Falsehood and calumny played their part. I was denounced and vilified. Everything was at stake. I simply had to speak and make the people understand, and that is how I got my training in oratory, and all the secret there is in whatever power of expression I may have.

In reading the history of slavery I studied the character of John Brown and he became my hero. I read the speeches of Wendell Phillips and was profoundly stirred by his marvelous powers. Once I heard him and was enthralled by his indescribable eloquence. He was far advanced in years, but I could see in his commanding presence and mellow and subdued tones how he must have blazed and flashed in the meridian of his powers.

At about the same time I first heard Robert G. Ingersoll. He was in my opinion the perfect master of the art of human speech. He combined all the graces, gifts and powers of expression, and stood upon the highest pinnacle of oratorical achievement.

Robert G. Ingersoll and Wendell Phillips were the two greatest orators of their time, and probably of all time. Their power sprang from their passion for freedom, for truth, for justice, for a world filled with light and with happy human beings. But for this divine passion neither would have scaled the sublime heights of immortal achievement. The sacred fire burned within them and when they were aroused it flashed from their eyes and rolled from their inspired lips in torrents of eloquence.

No man ever made a great speech on a mean subject. Slavery never inspired an immortal thought or utterance. Selfishness is dead to every art. The love of truth and the passion to serve it light every torch of real eloquence.

Had Ingersoll and Phillips devoted their lives to the practice of law for pay the divine fire within them would have burned to ashes and they would have died in mediocrity.

The highest there is in oratory is the highest there is in truth, in honesty, in morality. All the virtues combine in expressing themselves in beautiful words, poetic phrases, glowing periods, and moving eloquence.

The loftiest peaks rise from the lowest depths and their shining summits glorify their hidden foundations.

The highest eloquence springs from the lowliest sources and pleads trumpet-tongued for the children of the abyss.

Wendell Phillips was inspired by the scarred back, the pleading eyes, and the mute lips of chattel slavery and his tongue, eloquent with the lightning of Jehovah's wrath, became an avenging flame to scourge the horror of slavery from the earth.

Denial of one's better self seals the lips or pollutes them. Fidelity to conviction opens them and truth blossoms in eloquence.

The tongue is tipped with the flame that leaps from the altar-fire of the soul.

Ingersoll and Phillips were absolutely true to their convictions. They attacked monstrous evils and were hated and denounced. Had they yielded to the furies which assailed them they would have perished. But the fiercer the attacks upon them the stauncher they stood and the more eloquent and powerful they became. The truth fired their souls, flashed from their eyes, and inspired their lips.

There is no inspiration in evil and no power except for its own destruction.

He who aspires to master the art of expression must first of all consecrate himself completely to some great cause, and the greatest cause of all is the cause of humanity. He must learn to feel deeply and think clearly to express himself eloquently. He must be absolutely true to the best there is in him, if he has to stand alone.

Such natural powers as he may have should be cultivated by the study of history, science and literature. He must not only keep close to the people but remember that he is one of them, and not above the meanest. He must feel the wrongs of others so keenly that he forgets his own, and resolve to combat these wrongs with all the power at his command.

The most thrilling and inspiring oratory, the most powerful and impressive eloquence is the voice of the disinherited, the oppressed, the suffering and submerged; it is the voice of poverty and misery, of rags and crusts, of wretchedness and despair; the voice of humanity crying to the infinite; the voice that resounds throughout the earth and reaches heaven; the voice that awakens the conscience of the race and proclaims the truths that fill the world with light and liberty and love.

dec

JESUS, THE SUPREME LEADER. Coming Nation (Formerly Progressive Woman), March, 1914.

It matters little whether Jesus was born at Nazareth or Bethlehem. The accounts conflict, but the point is of no consequence.

It is of consequence, however, that He was born in a stable and cradled in a manger. This fact of itself, about which there is no question, certifies conclusively the proletarian character of Jesus Christ. Had His parents been other than poor working people—money-changers, usurers, merchants, lawyers, scribes, priests or other parasites—He would not have been delivered from His mother's womb on a bed of straw in a stable among asses and other animals.

Was Jesus divinely begotten? Yes, the same as every other babe ever born into the world. He was of miraculous origin the same as all the rest of mankind. The scriptural account of his "immaculate conception" is a beautiful myth, but scarcely more of a miracle than the conception of all other babes.

Jesus was not divine because he was less human than his fellowmen but for the opposite reason that he was supremely human, and it is this of which his divinity consists, the fullness and perfection of him as an intellectual, moral and spiritual human being.

The chronicles of his time and of later days are filled with contradictory and absurd stories about him and he has been disfigured and distorted by cunning priests to serve their knavish ends and by ignorant idolaters to give godly sanction to their blind bigotry and savage superstition, but there is no impenetrable myth surrounding the personality of Jesus Christ. He was not a legendary being or an allegorical figure, but as Bouck White and others have shown us, a flesh and blood Man in the fulness of his matchless powers and the completeness of his transcendent consecration.

To me Jesus Christ is as real, as palpitant and pervasive as a historic character as John Brown, Abraham Lincoln or Karl Marx. He has persisted in spite of two thousand years of theological emasculation to destroy his revolutionary personality, and is today the greatest moral force in the world.

The vain attempt persisted in through twenty centuries of ruling class interpolation, interpretation and falsification to make Jesus appear the divinely commissioned conservator of the peace and soother of the oppressed, instead of the master proletarian revolutionist and sower of the social whirlwind—the vain attempt to prostitute the name and teachings and example of the martyred Christ to the power of Mammon, the very power which had murdered him in cold blood, vindicates his transcendent genius and proclaims the immortality of his work.

Nothing is known of Jesus Christ as a lad except that at twelve his parents took him to Jerusalem, where he confounded the learned doctors by the questions he asked them. We have no knowledge as to what these questions were, but taking his lowly birth, his poverty and suffering into account, in contrast with the riches of Jerusalem which now dazzled his vision, and in the light of his subsequent career we are not left to conjecture as to the nature of the interrogation to which the inquisitive lad subjected the smug doctors in the temple.

There are but meagre accounts of the doings of Jesus until at a trifle over thirty he entered upon his public "ministry" and began the campaign of agitation and revolt he had been planning and dreaming through all the years of his yearning and burning adolescence. He was of the working class and loyal to it in every drop of his hot blood to the very hour of his death. He hated and denounced the rich and cruel exploiter as passionately as he loved and sympathized with his poor and suffering victims.

"I speak not of you all; I know whom I have chosen," was his class-conscious announcement to his disciples, all of whom were of the proletariat, not an exploiter or desirable citizen among them. No, not one! It was a working class movement he was organizing and a working class revolution he was preparing the way for.

"A new commandment I give unto you: That ye love one another; as I have loved you, that ye also love one another." This was the pith and core of all his pleading, all his preaching, and all his teaching—love one another, be brethren, make common cause, stand together, ye who labor to enrich the parasites and are yourselves in chains, and ye shall be free!

These words were addressed by Jesus not to the money-changers, the scribes and pharisees, the rich and respectable, but to the ragged undesirables of his own enslaved and suffering class. This appeal was to their class spirit, their class loyalty and their class solidarity.

Centuries later Karl Marx embodies the appeal in his famous manifesto and today it blazes forth in letters of fire as the watchword of the world-wide revolution: "*Workers of all countries unite: you have nothing to lose but your chains. You have a world to gain.*"

During the brief span of three years, embracing the whole period of his active life, from the time he began to stir up the people until "the scarlet robe and crown of thorns were put on him and he was crucified between two thieves," Jesus devoted all his time and all his matchless ability and energies to the suffering poor, and it would have been passing strange if they had not "heard him gladly."

He himself had no fixed abode and like the wretched, motley throng to whom he preached and poured out his great and loving heart, he was a poor wanderer on the face of the earth and "had not where to lay his head."

Pure communism was the economic and social gospel preached by Jesus Christ, and every act and utterance which may properly be ascribed to him conclusively affirms it. Private property was to his elevated mind and exalted soul a sacrilege and a horror; an insult to God and a crime against man.

The economic basis of his doctrine of brotherhood, and love is clearly demonstrated in the fact that under his leadership and teaching all his disciples "sold their possessions and goods, and parted them to all men, *as every man had need*," and that they "had all things in common."

"And they, continuing daily with one accord in the temple, and breaking bread from house to house, did eat their meat with gladness and singleness of heart."

This was the beginning of the mighty movement Jesus had launched for the overthrow of the empire of the Caesars and the emancipation of the crushed and miserable masses from the bestial misrule of the Roman tyrants.

It was above all a working class movement and was conceived and brought forth for no other purpose than to destroy class rule and set up the common people as the sole and rightful inheritors of the earth.

"Happy are the lowly for they shall inherit the earth."

Three short years of agitation by the incomparable Jesus was sufficient to stamp the proletarian movement he had inaugurated as the most formidable and portentous revolution in the annals of time. The ill-fated author could not long survive his stupendous mischief. The aim and inevitable outcome of this madman's teaching and agitation was too clearly manifest to longer admit of doubt.

The sodden lords of misrule trembled in their stolen finery, and then the word went forth that they must "get" the vagabond who had stirred up the people against them. The prototypes of Peabody, McPartland, Harry Orchard, et. al., were all ready for their base and treacherous performance and their thirty pieces of blood-stained silver. The priest of the Mammon worshipers gave it out that the Nazarene was spreading a false religion and that his pernicious teachings would corrupt the people, destroy the church, uproot the old faith, disrupt the family, break up the home, and overthrow society.

The lineal descendants of Caiaphas and Judas and the pharisees and money-changers of old are still parroting the same miserable falsehood to serve the same miserable ends, the only difference being that the brood of pious perverts now practice their degeneracy in the name of the Christ they betrayed and sold into crucifixion twenty centuries ago.

Jesus, after the most farcical trial and the most shocking travesty upon justice, was spiked to the cross at the gates of Jerusalem and his followers subjected to persecution, torture, exile and death. The movement he had inaugurated, fired by his unconquerable revolutionary spirit, persisted, however, through fire and slaughter, for three centuries and until the master class, realizing the futility of their efforts to stamp it out, basely betrayed it by pretending conversion to its teachings and reverence for its murdered founder, and from that time forth Christianity became the religion, so-called, of the pagan ruling class and the dead Christ was metamorphosed from the master revolutionist who was ignominiously slain, a martyr to his class, into the pious abstraction, the harmless theological divinity who died that John Pierpont Morgan could be "washed in the blood of the lamb" and countless generations of betrayed and deluded slaves kept blinded by superstition and content in their poverty and degradation.

Jesus was the grandest and loftiest of human souls—sun-crowned and God-inspired; a full-statured man, red-blooded and lion-hearted, yet

16

sweet and gentle as the noble mother who had given him birth.

He had the majesty and poise of a god, the prophetic vision of a seer, the great, loving heart of a woman, and the unaffected innocence and simplicity of a child.

This was and is the martyred Christ of the working class, the inspired evangel of the downtrodden masses, the world's supreme revolutionary leader, whose love for the poor and the children of the poor hallowed all the days of his consecrated life, lighted up and made forever holy the dark tragedy of his death, and gave to the ages his divine inspiration and his deathless name.

dec

SUSAN B. ANTHONY: A REMINISCENCE. Socialist Woman, January, 1909.

Twice only did I personally meet Susan B. Anthony, although I knew her well. The first time was at Terre Haute, Indiana, my home, in 1880, and the last time shortly before her death at her home at Rochester, New York. I can never forget the first time I met her. She impressed me as being a wonderfully strong character, self-reliant, thoroughly in earnest, and utterly indifferent to criticism.

There was never a time in my life when I was opposed to the equal suffrage of the sexes. I could never understand why woman was denied any right or opportunity that man enjoyed. Quite early, therefore, I was attracted to the woman suffrage movement. I had of course read of Susan B. Anthony and from the ridicule and contempt with which she was treated I concluded that she must be a strong advocate of, and doing effective work for, the rights of her sex. It was then that I determined, with the aid of Mrs. Ida Husted Harper, the brilliant writer, who afterward became her biographer, to arrange a series of meetings for Miss Anthony at Terre Haute.

In due course of time I received a telegram from Miss Anthony from Lafayette announcing the time of her arrival at Terre Haute and asking me to meet her at the station. I recognized the distinguished lady or, to be more exact, the notorious woman, the instant she stepped from the train. She was accompanied by Lily Devereaux Blake and other woman suffrage agitators and I proceeded to escort them to the hotel where I had arranged for their reception.

I can still see the aversion so unfeelingly expressed for this magnificent woman. Even my friends were disgusted with me for piloting such an "undesirable citizen" into the community. It is hard to understand, after all these years, how bitter and implacable the people were, especially the women, toward the leaders of this movement.

As we walked along the street I was painfully aware that Miss Anthony was an object of derision and contempt, and in my heart I resented it and later I had often to defend my position, which, of course, I was ever ready to do.

The meetings of Miss Anthony and her co-workers were but poorly attended and all but barren of results. Such was the loathing of the community for a woman who dared to talk in public about "woman's rights" that people would not go to see her even to satisfy their curiosity. She was simply not to be tolerated and it would not have required any great amount of egging-on to have excited the people to drive her from the community.

To all of this Miss Anthony, to all appearance, was entirely oblivious. She could not have helped noticing it for there were those who thrust their insults upon her but she gave no sign and bore no resentment.

I can see her still as she walked along, neatly but carelessly attired, her bonnet somewhat awry, mere trifles which were scarcely noticed, if at all, in the presence of her splendid womanhood. She seemed absorbed completely in her mission. She could scarcely speak of anything else. The rights and wrongs of her sex seemed to completely possess her and to dominate all her thoughts and acts.

On the platform she spoke with characteristic earnestness and at times with such intensity as to awe her audience, if not compel conviction. She had an inexhaustible fund of information in regard to current affairs, and dates and data for all things. She spoke with great rapidity and forcefulness; her command of language was remarkable and her periods were all well-rounded and eloquently delivered. No thoughtful person could hear her without being convinced of her honesty and the purity of her motive. Her face fairly glowed with the spirit of her message and her soul was in her speech.

But the superb quality, the crowning virtue she possessed, was her moral heroism.

Susan B. Anthony had this quality in an eminent degree. She fearlessly faced the ignorant multitude or walked unafraid among those who scorned her. She had the dignity of perfect self-reliance without a shadow of conceit to mar it. She was a stern character, an uncompromising personality, but she had the heart of a woman and none more tender ever throbbed for the weak and the oppressed of earth.

No leader of any crusade was ever more fearless, loyal or uncompromising than Susan B. Anthony and not one ever wrought more unselfishly or under greater difficulties for the good of her kind and for the progress of the race.

I did not see Miss Anthony again until I shook hands with her at the close of my address in Rochester, but a short time before she passed to other realms. She was the same magnificent woman, but her locks had whitened and her kindly features bore the traces of age and infirmity.

Her life-work was done and her sun was setting!

How beautiful she seemed in the quiet serenity of her sunset!

Twenty-five years before she drank to its dregs the bitter cup of persecution, but now she stood upon the heights, a sad smile lighting her sweet face, amidst the acclaims of her neighbors and the plaudits of the world.

Susan B. Anthony freely consecrated herself to the service of humanity; she was a heroine in the highest sense and her name deserves a place among the highest on the scroll of the immortals.

dec

LOUIS TIKAS—LUDLOW'S HERO AND MARTYR. Appeal to Reason, September 4, 1915.

"And now that the cloud settled upon Saint Antoine which a momentary gleam had driven from his sacred countenance, the darkness of it was heavy—cold, dirt, sickness, ignorance and want, were the lords in waiting on the saintly presence—nobles of great power all of them; but most especially the last. Samples of a people that had undergone a terrible grinding and regrinding in the mill, and certainly not in the fabulous mill which ground old people young, shivered at every corner.... The mill which had worked them down was the mill that grinds young people old; the children had ancient faces and grave voices; and upon them, and upon the grown faces, and plowed into every furrow of age and coming up afresh, was the sign, Hunger. It was prevalent everywhere. Hunger was pushed out of the tall houses, in the wretched clothing that hung upon the poles and lines; hunger was patched into them with straw and rags and wood and paper; hunger was repeated in every modicum of fire-wood that the man sawed off; hunger stared down from the smokeless chimneys, and started up from the filthy street that had no offal, among its refuse, of anything to eat. Hunger was the inscription on the baker's shelves, written in every small loaf of his scanty stock of bad bread; at the sausage-shop, in every dead-dog preparation that was offered for sale. Hunger rattled its dry bones among the roasting chestnuts in the turned cylinder; hunger was shred into atoms in every farthing of husky chips of potato, fried with some reluctant drops of oil.

"Its abiding place was in all things fitted to it. A narrow winding street, full of offense and stench, with other narrow winding streets diverging, all peopled by rags and nightcaps, and all smelling of rags and nightcaps, and all visible things with a brooding look upon them that looked ill. In the hunted air of the people there was yet some wild-beast thought of the possibility of turning at bay. Depressed and slinking though they were, eyes of fire were not wanting among them; nor compressed lips, white with what they suppressed; nor foreheads knitted into the likeness of the gallows-rope they mused about enduring or inflicting."—*A Tale of Two Cities*.

In these ghastly colors Charles Dickens painted the picture of poverty

21

and its starving victims in France on the eve of the French revolution, and yet, "every wind that blew over France shook the rags of the scarecrows in vain, for the birds, fine of song and feather took no warning." Then the storm broke and the pent-up furies were unleashed; the day of reckoning had come at last and the crimes of the centuries, inflicted without mercy upon the long-suffering people, were wiped out in the hearts' blood of their aristocratic and profligate oppressors and despoilers.

The bloody revolution of a century and a quarter ago in France fills uncounted pages in the world's history, but its terrible warning to the lords of misrule and despoilers of the people has been in vain. Today as ever the greed and avarice of the ruling class blind them to their impending fate and drive them to their inevitable doom.

In the state of Colorado in "our own free America" the conditions that make for savage and bloody revolution are ripening with incredible rapidity and the lurid handwriting of fate is already upon the wall, but the Rockefellers and their capitalist cohorts, stricken blind as the penalty of their insatiate greed, are unable to see it.

That the monstrous crime of Ludlow, the fiendish destruction of the tented village, the wanton killing of the homeless, hunted, hopeless victims—half-clad, famishing, terror-stricken and defenseless—bludgeoned, bullied, shot down like dogs, and their wives and suckling babes roasted in pits before their eyes—that this appalling massacre, without a parallel in history, did not infuriate the suffering and persecuted victims of capitalism's worse than satanic ferocity, fire their blood with the tiger-thirst for revenge, and drench the despotic and shameless state with blood is one of the miracles of patience and submissiveness of the exploited, downtrodden, suffering masses.

The tragic story of Ludlow, the hideous nightmare of the infernal regions of the Rocky(feller) Mountains—written in the violated wombs of shrieking mothers and the spattered life-drops of their murdered babes—has yet to be traced on history's ineffaceable pages. The blood of the twenty-three innocents who perished there will be the holy fount of the writer's inspiration whose fire-tipped pen will give to the world this tragic and thrilling epic of the embattled miners in the mountain ramparts of Rockefellerado.

In the story of Ludlow, Louis Tikas, the intrepid leader, the loyal comrade, the noble-hearted Greek who fell the victim of gunmen-brutes in military uniform while pleading that the women and children be spared, takes on the robes of deity and joins the martyrs and heroes of history. The rifle-butt that crushed his noble head and silenced his brave and tender heart gave his soul to the cause he loved and his name to the ages.

The lion-hearted Greek is at rest, but the cause he lived and died for goes on forever!

Louis Tikas was educated, cultured and refined, a graduate of the University of Athens; yea, he was more than that, he was a MAN! His heart was true as his brain was clear; he followed the truth and he loved justice; he sided with the weak and ministered to the suffering, even as his elder brother had in the days when other pharisees crucified the Son of Man for loving his despoiled and despised fellow-men.

Louis Tikas made Ludlow holy as Jesus Christ made Calvary!

He was the loyal leader of the persecuted colony; the trusted keeper of the tented village. He was loved by every man, woman and child, and feared only by the fanged wolves and hyenas that threatened to ravage the flock.

Strong as a giant yet gentle as a child; utterly fearless yet without bravado, this great and loving soul cast his lot with the exiled slaves of the pits and kept his vigil over the defenseless women and children of the village as a loving mother might over the fledglings of her brood.

Is it strange that they loved him, trusted him, and that in the hour of their deadly peril they looked to him to shield them from their brutish ravishers?

In this tragic hour Louis Tikas measured up to the supreme stature of his noble manhood. He knew his time had come and with a smile upon his lips and without a tremor in his sinews, he faced his cruel fate. He asked no quarter for himself, but only begged that mothers and babes be spared; and with this touching plea upon his lips and the love of his people in his soul and beaming from his eyes, he was struck down by the hired assassins of the Arch-Pharisee and passed to martyrdom and immortality.

dec

THE LITTLE LORDS OF LOVE. Progressive Woman, December, 1910.

The children are to me a perpetual source of wonder and delight. How keen they are, how alert, and how comprehending!

The sweet children of the Socialist movement—the little lords of light and love—keep my heart warm and my purpose true. The raggedest and dirtiest of them all is to me an angel of light. I have seen them, the proletarian little folks, swarming up out of the sub-cellars and down from the garrets of the tenements and I have watched them with my heart filled with pity and my eyes overflowing with tears. Their very glee seemed tragic beyond words.

Born within the roar of the ocean their tiny feet are never kissed by the eager surf, nor their wan cheeks made ruddy by the vitalizing breezes of the sea.

Not for them—the flotsam and jetsam upon the social tides—are the rosy hours of babyhood, the sweet, sweet joys of childhood. They are the heirs of the social filth and disease of capitalism and death marks them at what should be the dewy dawn of birth, and they wither and die—without having been born. Their cradle is their coffin and their birth robe their winding sheet.

The Socialist movement is the first in all history to come to the rescue of childhood and to set free the millions of little captives. And they realize it and incarnate the very spirit of the movement and shout aloud their joy as it marches on to victory.

The little revolutionists in Socialist parades know what they are there for, and in our audiences they are wide awake to the very last word. They know, too, when to applaud, and the speaker who fails to enthuse them is surely lacking in some vital element of his speech.

At the close of a recent meeting in a western state the stage was crowded with eager comrades shaking hands and offering congratulations. My hand was suddenly gripped from below. I glanced down and a little comrade just about big enough to stand alone looked straight up into my eyes and said with all the frankness and sincerity of a child: "That was a great speech you made and I love you; keep this to remember me by." And he handed me a little nickle-plated whistle, his sole tangible possession, and with it all the wealth of his pure and unpolluted child-love, which filled my heart and moved me to tears.

In just that moment that tiny proletaire filled my measure to overflowing and consecrated me with increased strength and devotion to the great movement that is destined to rescue the countless millions of disinherited babes and give them the earth and all the fulness thereof as their patrimony forever.

The sweetest, tenderest, most pregnant words uttered by the proletaire of Galilee were: "Suffer little children, and forbid them not, to come unto me; for of such is the kingdom of heaven."

dec

THE COPPOCK BROTHERS: HEROES OF HARPER'S FERRY.
Appeal to Reason, May 23, 1914.

"O, patience, felon of the hour! Over thy ghastly gallows-tree Shall climb the vine of Liberty, With ripened fruit and fragrant flower."

So wrote William Dean Howells, then a rising young poet and author in Columbus, Ohio, in November, 1859, on the eve of John Brown's execution at Charleston, Va. In the month before, on the night of October 16th, John Brown, at the head of twenty-one men, sixteen of whom were white and five black, marched on Harper's Ferry and delivered the attack that sent his body to the gallows and his soul to immortal glory.

The heroic blood of old Brown himself flowed in the veins of all his twenty-one intrepid young followers. There was not a coward among them. Three of them were Brown's own sons and two others were near relatives.

Brown was fifty-nine; his adjutant general twenty-four. All his followers were young men, some of them barely of age.

When Colonel Richard J. Hinton, who followed John Brown in Kansas, heard of the intended raid on Harper's Ferry, he said to Kagi, the stripling adjutant general: "You'll all be killed." "Yes, I know it, Hinton," was the ready reply, "but the result will be worth the sacrifice."

Kagi was said to resemble "a divinity student rather than a warrior," and when taunted by an adversary, he answered, "We will endure the shadow of dishonor, but not the stain of guilt."

"These words of John Henry Kagi," wrote Hinton, "expressed the spirit of John Brown's men and, in an especial sense, the character of the young and brilliant man who fell riddled with bullets into the Shenandoah. Thirty miles below, the blood-tinged stream flowed through the lands of his father's family."

Spartan souls were these who marched on Harper's Ferry that fateful night, there to strike a blow at the cost of their lives that was destined to make Harper's Ferry more famed than Waterloo—a blow that was to emancipate a race and change abruptly the whole current of American history.

"Down the still road, dim white in the moonlight, and amid the chill

27

of the October night, went the little band, silent and sober."

The twenty-one young heroes who followed old John Brown on that historic night were of the exalted type that Emerson described: "When souls reach a certain clearness of perception, they accept a knowledge and motive without selfishness."

It is related that when Garibaldi was organizing his army of liberation in Italy, he was asked what inducements he had to offer to new recruits. Promptly the rebel chieftain answered: "Poverty, hardships, battles, wounds, and—victory!"

That was all Captain Brown had to offer his devoted followers, with crushing defeat instead of victory at the end, and yet they enlisted with a zeal that could not have been surpassed if the world's most coveted prizes had been their promised reward.

Think of the utter abnegation, unselfishness and loftiness of purpose of that valiant little band who marched deliberately into the jaws of hell that October night to break the fetters of a despised and alien race! How many of their detractors and persecutors were animated by motives so pure and exalted?

No wonder that Victor Hugo protested so eloquently, albeit in vain, against John Brown's execution. "Think of a republic," he indignantly exclaimed, "murdering a liberator!" and when the bloody deed was done the illustrious Frenchman flung back the prophetic challenge: "The time will come when your John Brown will be greater than your George Washington."

Among Brown's men in the attack on Harper's Ferry there were two Quaker brothers, Edwin and Barclay Coppock, stalwart young abolitionists from Iowa, whose unfaltering devotion to the cause, heroic self-sacrifice and tragic death constitute one of the most thrilling and inspiring chapters in American history.

Edwin, the elder brother, was captured with his leader and shared his fate on the gallows. Barclay made good his escape with Owen Brown, to be killed later as a lieutenant, while recruiting a regiment for the war which had then actually begun.

Edwin and Barclay Coppock were born of Quaker parents near Salem, Ohio, Edwin on June 30, 1835, and Barclay on January 4, 1839, so that Edwin was 24 and Barclay not quite 21 when the attack was made on

Harper's Ferry.

Salem was at that time the center of abolitionism in that section. It was settled by Quakers and they were strongly anti-slavery in sentiment. The headquarters of the "Western Anti-Slavery Society" was located here, and here also was published the "Anti-Slavery Bugle," official organ of the movement, of which Benjamin S. Jones, Oliver Johnson and Warren R. Robertson were editors. They waged uncompromising warfare against slavery, attacked the United States constitution as it was then being interpreted, and denounced the churches that would not come out openly in favor of abolition. They were called "Disunion Abolitionists," "Covenanters" and "Infidels." But nothing daunted, they demanded the unconditional surrender of the slave power.

During one of the annual conventions held at the Hicksite Friends' church in Salem and in the midst of a violent speech that was being delivered against the encroachments of slavery on Northern soil under the fugitive slave law, an excited man entered with a telegram in his hand and announced breathlessly that the four o'clock train, due in thirty minutes, had aboard of it a southern man and his wife and a colored slave girl as a nurse. It was at once proposed that they proceed to the depot in a body and meet the train on arrival. The meeting was hastily adjourned. Intense enthusiasm prevailed. They marched to the depot cheering as they went and when the train pulled in they boarded it, took the slave girl without protest from her master and mistress and marched back to the hall with her in triumph. The liberated girl was christened Abby Kelly Salem, in honor of Abby Kelly Foster, one of the speakers at the convention, and the city of Salem. The girl grew up to splendid womanhood and was highly esteemed by all who knew her.

The old town hall, still standing, is where many an anti-slavery meeting was held in that day. The most stirring and eloquent appeals were made in this old meeting house by such noted abolitionists as William Lloyd Garrison, Wendell Phillips, Susan B. Anthony, Parker Pillsbury, Horace Mann, John Pierpont, Gerrit Smith, Fred Douglas, Lucretia Mott, Elizabeth Cady Stanton, Owen Lovejoy, Abby Kelly Foster, George Thompson of England, Ralph Waldo Emerson, Robert Collyer, John P. Hale and many others.

The walls of the old town hall resounded daily and nightly with the patriotism and love of freedom of Quaker Salem.

It was in this atmosphere and under the influence of these impassioned teachings that the Coppock brothers, sons of a nearby Quaker farmer, grew up to young manhood. It had been ingrained into their very nature that all men were created equal and that slavery was a crime against God and man, and with this conviction they resolved to shoulder their muskets and go out and fight to liberate the slaves.

The family moved to Iowa in the meantime and it was here that these young Quaker enthusiasts first met John Brown, who was then waging his warfare against slavery in the free soil conflict in that state. From now on their die was cast. They would follow the grim old chief to victory or death. It proved to be death for them both and when it came they met it with a calmness and resignation possible only to the loftiest heroism.

Barclay Coppock was barely twenty years of age at the time of the attack on Harper's Ferry. His escape was almost a miracle. A heavy reward was offered for him dead or alive. After weeks of the most intense privation and suffering, lying concealed in the brush during the day and moving chiefly by night, he picked his way back to the family home at Springdale, Iowa. The governor of Virginia issued a requisition for his return, which was not granted. The young men at Springdale and that vicinity organized to protect young Coppock and served notice on the Virginia officers who were on his track that "Springdale is in arms and is prepared at a half hour's notice to give them a reception of 200 shots."

In the following spring Barclay returned to Salem and here again the Virginia authorities renewed their efforts to capture him. But Barclay, now among his old neighbors and friends, defied them. He sent word to the officers in pursuit of him as to where he might be found, but they wisely refrained from attempting to take him.

It was at this time that Barclay was a guest of the Bonsall family of Salem, the elder Bonsall being one of the leading abolitionists of that day. Charles Bonsall, his son, who still lives at Salem, knew the Coppock brothers well and has a distinct recollection of Barclay's stay at his father's home.

"During Barclay's sojourn at our home," writes Charles Bonsall in a personal letter, "a detective of Salem heard of his being in our neighborhood and boasted of his intention to arrest Barclay and secure the reward there was on his head. Barclay heard of the boast and wrote a letter to the detective informing him that he might select five other men and he would meet them all single-handed and alone at any point outside the city that he might name, and they could have the privilege of capturing him and securing the reward. The detective did not undertake the job.... Barclay Coppock never knew what fear was. When a boy in his teens he often went to the woods and slept alone all night on the ground, under the trees, from the sheer love of adventure. He was the best shot with his eight-inch Colt I ever saw. On one occasion, in his uncle's woods south of Salem, with his revolver, he shot a grey squirrel from a big oak tree and put two more balls through its body before it reached the ground. His nerves were as calm and steady in a fight as in his sleep, and while with us his trusted "navy" was always strapped under his coat, while in his coat-pocket he carried a small pistol ready for any emergency at close quarters. It would have been impossible to capture him alive."

Barclay Coppock's escape and the execution of his brother but intensified his hatred and horror of slavery. He was now thoroughly aroused and intent upon plunging anew into the fight. Returning to Iowa, and convinced that civil war was now inevitable, he prepared actively for the conflict.

"Now comes one of those remarkable facts of super-epochal history," continues Bonsall, "which go to show that when revolutionary periods focalize, revolutions in public sentiment are brought about in almost a twinkling. In the spring of 1861, just about one year from the time the United States Government was offering a reward of one thousand dollars for Barclay Coppock, dead or alive, the same government lifted its hat and humbly bowed to him, and begged him to accept a first lieutenant's commission in Company C, Third Kansas volunteers. He accepted the commission and at once proceeded to organize his company. Captain Allen of Ashtabula of the same company, came to Salem to recruit volunteers and the writer, together with half a score of other abolition boys, enlisted in Coppock's company.... Soon after Lieutenant Coppock was on his way from Springdale to Fort Leavenworth to join his regiment there. The rebels in Missouri, hearing of his coming, burned the railroad bridge across the Little Platte river near St. Joseph, and the train carrying the troops was precipitated into the river in the darkness of night and brave Lieutenant Coppock was killed in the wreck."

31

Thus perished, still in his boyhood, as heroic a heart, as noble a soul, as ever gave up his life in the cause of freedom. Had he been spared he would without doubt have become one of the famed heroes of the war of the rebellion.

Edwin Coppock was executed from the same gallows as his old chief, but two weeks later. His trial, like that of Brown, was a farce. Conviction, sentence and execution of all of Brown's men that were captured was a foregone conclusion.

While awaiting the execution of his sentence, Edwin wrote to Mrs. Brown, wife of his dead leader:

"I was with your sons when they fell. Oliver lived but a very few moments after he was shot. He spoke no word, but yielded calmly to his fate. Watson was shot at ten o'clock Monday morning and died about three o'clock Monday afternoon.... After we were taken prisoners he was placed in the guardhouse with me. He complained of the hardness of the bench on which he was lying. I begged hard for a bed for him, or even a blanket, but could obtain none. I took off my coat and placed it under him and held his head in my lap, in which position he died without a groan or struggle."

In a letter to friends in Iowa, under date of November 22d, three weeks before his execution, he wrote:

"Eleven of our little band are sleeping now in their bloody garments with the cold earth above them. Braver men never lived; truer men to their plighted word never banded together."

Rigidly true to their convictions were all these young heroes. Not one showed the white feather in the last hour. Serenely and without a quiver each of them met his cruel fate.

John Brown had trained up his men in the strictest discipline. Not a drop of liquor was allowed in his camp. Tobacco was tabooed. Profane language was forbidden.

These men were in deadly earnest and their asceticism attested their single-hearted fidelity to their cause. They were profoundly convinced that slavery was a national crime and that it was their patriotic duty, at whatever cost, to wipe that insufferable stigma from the land.

And who shall say that they were not right; or that they forfeited their brave lives in vain?

A few days before the gallows claimed him, John Brown wrote to his family, "I feel no consciousness of guilt and I am perfectly certain that very soon no member of the family will feel any possible disposition to blush on my account."

The Coppock brothers were typical of all the brave young abolitionists who banded together to strike a blow that rocked this nation as if Jehovah in his wrath had laid hold on it. Quaker lads, "grave, quiet, reserved, even rustic in their ways," they lived bravely up to their convictions and sealed their devotion to the cause of freedom with their precious young life blood.

The noble character of Edwin Coppock is revealed in the following pathetic letter written to his uncle on the eve of his execution. There is no bitterness in his heart at the last hour. Like the great Galilean who also perished for sympathizing with the lowly and oppressed, he was calm and resigned in the presence of his fate. Like all such souls he was gifted with prophetic vision, as his letter shows:

Charleston, December 13, 1859.

Joshua Coppock:

My Dear Uncle—I seat myself by the stand to write for the first and last time to thee and thy dear family. Though far from home and overtaken by misfortune, I have not forgotten you. Your generous hospitality towards me, during my short stay with you last spring, is stamped indelibly upon my heart, and also the generosity bestowed upon my brother who now wanders, an outcast from his native land. But thank God, he is free. I am thankful it is I who has to suffer instead of him.

The time may come when he will remember me. And the time may come when he may still further remember the cause in which I die. Thank God the principles of the cause in which we were engaged will not die with me and my brave comrades. They will spread wider and wider and gather strength with each hour that passes. The voice of truth will echo through our land, bringing conviction to the erring and adding members to the glorious army who will follow its banner. The cause of everlasting truth and justice will go on conquering and to conquer until our broad and beautiful land shall rest beneath the banner of freedom. I had fondly hoped to live to see the principles of the Declaration of Independence fully realized. I had hoped to see the dark stain of slavery blotted from our land, and the libel of our boasted freedom erased, when we can say in truth that our beloved country is the land of the free and the home of the brave; but that cannot be.

I have heard my sentence passed; my doom is sealed. But two more short days remains for me to fulfill my earthly destiny. But two brief days between me and eternity. At the expiration of those two days I shall stand upon the scaffold to take my last look of earthly scenes. But that scaffold has but little dread for me, for I honestly believe I am innocent of any crime justifying such punishment. But by the taking of my life and the lives of my comrades, Virginia is but hastening on that glorious day, when the slave will rejoice in his freedom and say, "I, too, am a man, and am groaning no more under the yoke of oppression."

But I must now close. Accept this short scrawl as a remembrance of me. Give my love to all the family. Kiss little Joey for me. Remember me to all my relatives and friends. And now farewell for the last time.

From thy nephew, EDWIN COPPOCK.

Two days later the slave state of Virginia hung Edwin Coppock by the neck until he was dead. The gallant John E. Cook went to the scaffold with him. The account says:

"After the cap had been placed on their heads, Coppock turned toward Cook and stretched forward his hand as far as possible. At the same time Cook said, 'Stop a minute—where is Edwin's hand?' They then shook hands cordially and Cook said, 'God bless you.' The calm and collected manner of both was very marked.... They both exhibited the most unflinching firmness, saying nothing, with the exception of bidding farewell to the ministers and the sheriff."

More than half a century has passed since John Brown and his faithful followers gave up their lives to set the black men free, but history has yet to do them justice. Some day the hatred and prejudice will all have died away and then these men, summoned to the bar of enlightened judgment, will be crowned as the greatest heroes in American history.

dec

THE SOCIAL SPIRIT. Appeal to Reason.

We need to grow out of the selfish, sordid, brutal spirit of individualism which still lurks even in Socialists and is responsible for the strife and contention which prevail where there should be concord and good will. The social spirit and the social conscience must be developed and govern our social relations before we shall have any social revolution.

If there are any among whom the social spirit should find its highest expression and who should be bound fast in its comradely embrace and give to the world the example of its elevating and humanizing influence, it is the Socialists. They of all others have come to realize the hardening and brutalizing effect of capitalist individualism in the awful struggle for existence and it is to them a cause of unceasing rejoicing that they live at a time in the world's historic development when the very conditions which resulted from this age-long struggle forbid its continuance and proclaim its approaching termination.

The rule of individualism which has governed society since the days of primitive communism has effectually restrained the moral and spiritual development of the race. It has brought out the baser side of men's nature and set them against each other as if the plan of creation had designed them to be mortal enemies.

  *   *   *   *

Typical capitalists are barren of the social spirit. The very nature of the catch-as-catch-can encounter in which they are engaged makes them wary and suspicious, if not downright hateful of each other, and the latent good that is in them dies for the want of incentive to express itself.

The other day I saw two such capitalists shake hands. It was pitiable. Their hearts had no part in the purely perfunctory ceremony. They happened to meet and could not avoid each other. And so they mechanically touched each other's reluctant hands, standing at right angles to each other for a moment—not face to face—and then passing on without either looking the other in the eyes.

This cold and heartless ceremony typified the relation begotten of capitalist individualism in which men's interests are competitive and antagonistic and in which each instinctively looks out for himself and is on the alert to take every possible advantage of his fellow-man.

The result of this system is inevitably a race of Ishmaelites.

How differently two Socialist comrades shake hands! Their hearts are in their palms and the joy of greeting is in their eyes. They have the social spirit. Their interests are mutual and their aspirations kindred. If one happens to be strong and the other weak, the stronger shares the weakness and the weaker shares the strength of his comrade. The base thought of taking a mean advantage, one of the other, does not darken their minds or harden their hearts. They are joined together in the humanizing bonds of fellowship. They multiply each other and they rejoice in their comradely kinship. The best there is in each, and not the worst, as in the contact of individualism, is appealed to and brought forth for the benefit of both.

What an elevating, enlarging and satisfying relation!

And this is the "dead level" of mediocrity and servitude to which we are to sink when this relation becomes universal among men as it will in the International Socialist Republic!

So at least we are told by those who in the present system have acquired the instincts and impulses of animals of prey in the development of their imagined superiority by draining the veins and wrecking the lives of their vanquished competitors, but we are not impressed by the virtues of the system of which they stand as the shining examples.

    *   *   *   *

Thru all the ages past men, civilized men, so-called, have been at each other's throats in the struggle for existence, and the spirit of individualism this struggle has begotten, the spirit of hard, sordid, brutal selfishness, has filled this world with unutterable anguish and woe.

But at last the end of the reign of anarchistic individualism is in sight. The social forces at work are undermining and destroying it and soon its knell will be sounded to the infinite joy of an emancipated world.

The largest possible expression of the social spirit should be fostered and encouraged in the Socialist movement and among Socialists themselves.

In spite of the hindrances which beset us in our present environments and relations, we may yet cultivate this spirit assiduously to our increasing mutual good and to the good of our great movement.

In our propaganda, in the discussion of our tactical and other differences and in all our other activities, the larger faith that true comradeship inspires should prevail between us. We need to be more patient, more kindly, more tolerant, more sympathetic, helpful and encouraging to one another, and less suspicious, less envious, and less contentious, if we are to educate and impress the people by our example, and by the effect of our teachings upon ourselves win them to our movement, and realize our dream of universal freedom and social righteousness.

dec

ROOSEVELT AND HIS REGIME. Appeal to Reason, April 20, 1907.

The only time in my life I ever saw Theodore Roosevelt was years before he became president of the United States. I was aboard of a train in the far west, where Roosevelt was then said to be following ranch life, and as he and several companions in cowboy costume entered the car at a station stop, he was pointed out to me. I did not like him. The years since have not altered that feeling of aversion except to accentuate it.

I have since seen the nation mad with hero worship over this man Roosevelt, but I have not been impressed by it. Very "great" men sometimes shrivel into very small ones and finally vanish in oblivion in the short space of a single generation.

The American people are more idolatrous than any "heathen" nation on earth. They worship their popular "heroes," while they last, with passionate frenzy, and with equal madness do they hunt down the sane "fools" who vainly try to teach them sense. Theodore Roosevelt and George Dewey as "heroes" and Wendell Phillips and John Brown as "fools" are notable illustrations. American history is filled with them.

But my personal dislike of the cowboy in imitation who has since become president, however justifiable, would scarcely warrant a public attack upon his official character, and this review, being of such a nature, is inspired, as will appear, by entirely different motives.

There are those, and they constitute a great majority of the American people, who stand in awe of their president, supposedly their servant, but in fact their master; they speak of him with a kind of reverential adulation as a lordly personage, a superior being to be looked up to and worshiped rather than a fellowman to be respected and loved. There are others who betray equal ignorance in a more vulgar fashion by coarse tirades for which there is often as little excuse as there is for the extreme adulation.

Regarding the president of the United States, as I do, simply as a citizen and fellowman, the same as any other, I shall speak of him and his acts free alike from awe and malice, and if I place him in the public pillory, where he has placed so many others, to be seen and despised of men, it will be from a sense that his official acts, so often in flat denial of his profession, merit the execration of honest men.

In arraigning President Roosevelt and his administration I have no private spite nor personal grudge to satisfy, but an obligation to redeem and a principle to vindicate.

I shall go about it as I would any other moral duty, asking no favors and prepared to accept all consequences.

In the first place, I charge President Roosevelt with being a hypocrite, the most consummate that ever occupied the executive seat of the nation. His profession of pure politics is false, his boasted moral courage the bluff of a bully and his "square deal" a delusion and a sham.

Theodore Roosevelt is mainly for Theodore Roosevelt and incidentally for such others as are also for the same distinguished gentleman, first, last and all the time. He is a smooth and slippery politician, swollen purple with self-conceit; he is shrewd enough to gauge the stupidity of the masses and unscrupulous enough to turn it into hero worship. This constitutes the demagogue, and he is that in superlative degree.

Only a few days ago he appeared in a characteristic role. Rushing into the limelight, as necessary to him as breath, he shrieked that he and "Root" were "horrified" because of certain scandalous and revolting charges made by one of his own former political chums. Of course, he and "Root" of Tweed fame, the foxiest "fixer" of them all, were "horrified" because of the shock to their political virtue, but it so happened that the horror took effect only when they found themselves uncovered. The taking of Harriman's boodle for corruptly electing him president and the use of the stolen insurance funds for the same criminal purpose did not "horrify" the president and "Root," nor would they be "horrified" yet if they had not been caught red-handed in the act with the booty upon their persons.

The cry of the exposed malefactor and all his pack of yelpers that he is the victim of a "plot" by his own friends and supporters, the very gentlemen (sic) who furnished him with free special trains, paid his campaign expenses and in fact bought the presidency for him, is so palpably false as to be absolutely ridiculous and only brings into bolder relief the hypocrisy and fraud it was designed to conceal.

This much is preliminary to the extraordinary official conduct of the president which has "horrified" not only its victims but millions of others, and now prompts this review and protest.

Something over a year ago Charles Moyer, William Haywood and George Pettibone, of Colorado, leading officials of the Western Federation of Miners, were overpowered and kidnaped by a gang of thugs and torn from their families at night by conspiracy of two degenerate governors and another notorious criminal acting for the Mine and Smelter Trust, one of the most stupendous aggregations of force and plunder in all America.

Every decent man and woman was "horrified" by this infamy and the whole working class of the nation cried out against it.

Was Roosevelt also "horrified"?

Yes!

Because the Mine and Smelter Trust had kidnaped three citizens of the republic?

Oh, no!

The three citizens were only working cattle and he never had any other conception of them.

He was "horrified" because the Mine and Smelter Trust, unclean birds that feather their nests, especially in Colorado, with legislatures and United States senatorships, had not killed instead of kidnaping their victims.

Then and there Theodore Roosevelt disgraced himself and his high office, and his cruel and cowardly act will load his name with odium as long as it is remembered.

The Mine and Smelter Trust had put up the funds and used its vast machinery for Roosevelt, and now Roosevelt must serve it even to the extent of upholding criminals, approving kidnaping and murdering its helpless victims.

When Roosevelt stepped out of the White House and called Moyer, Haywood and Pettibone *murderers*, men he had never seen and did not know; men who had never been tried, never convicted and whom every law of the land presumed innocent until proven guilty, he fell a million miles beneath where Lincoln stood, and there he grovels today with his political crimes, one after another, finding him out and pointing at him their accusing fingers.

No president of the United States has ever descended to such depths as has Roosevelt to serve his law-defying and crime-inciting masters.

40

The act is simply scandalous and without a parallel in American history.

What right has Theodore Roosevelt to prejudge American citizens, pronounce their guilt and hand them over to the hangman? In a pettifogging lawyer such an act would be infamous; in the president of the nation it becomes monstrous and staggers belief.

All that Roosevelt knows about Moyer, Haywood and Pettibone he knows from his friends, their kidnapers.

The millions of working men and women, embracing practically every labor union in America, count for nothing with him. He is not now standing for their votes. He is fulfilling his obligation to the gentlemen (!) who put up the coin that elected him; paying off the mortgage they hold upon his administration.

Theodore Roosevelt is swift to brand other men who even venture to disagree with him as liars. He, according to himself, is immaculate and infallible.

The greatest liar is he who sees only liars in others.

When Theodore Roosevelt, president of the United States, denounced Charles Moyer, William Haywood and George Pettibone as murderers, he uttered a lie as black and damnable, a calumny as foul and atrocious as ever issued from a human throat. The men he thus traduced and vilified, sitting in their prison cells for having dutifully served their fellow-workers and having spurned the bribes of their masters, transcend immeasurably the man in the White House, who, with the cruel malevolence of a barbarian, has pronounced their doom.

A thousand times rather would I be one of those men in Ada county jail than Theodore Roosevelt in the White House at Washington.

Had these men accepted, with but a shadow of the eagerness Roosevelt displayed, the debauching funds of the trust pirates, they would not now languish in felons' cells.

The same brazen robbers of the people and corrupters of the body politic who put Moyer, Haywood and Pettibone in jail, also put Theodore Roosevelt in the White House.

This accounts for his prostituting the high office Lincoln honored and resorting to methods that would shame a Bowery ward-heeler.

Moyer, Haywood and Pettibone are not murderers; it is a ghastly lie, and I denounce it in the name of law and in the name of justice. I know these men, these sons of toil; I know their hearts, their guileless nature and their rugged honesty. I love and honor them and shall fight for them while there is breath in my body.

Here and now I challenge Theodore Roosevelt. He is guilty of high crimes and deserves impeachment.

Let him do his worst. I denounce him and defy him.

During my recent visit at Washington I learned from those who know him what they think of Roosevelt. Among newspaper men he is literally despised. Their true feeling is not apparent in what they write, for they know that the slightest offense to the president is *lese majeste* and means instantaneous decapitation.

For the second time, Theodore Roosevelt, president of the United States, has now publicly convicted Moyer, Haywood and Pettibone. He has not pronounced condemnation upon Harry Thaw, or any rich man charged with murder. He has, however, made a postmaster of a man at Chicago charged by the Chicago *Tribune* with having shot another man in a midnight brawl over disreputable women, and then used his influence to make the same man mayor of that city.

Moyer, Haywood and Pettibone, the three workingmen kidnaped by the Mine and Smelter Trust, have now been in jail fourteen months; they have not been tried, but twice condemned by President Roosevelt, the last time but a few days ago, in connection with Harriman, his former political pal and financial backer. These men are in prison cells, their bodies in manacles and their lips sealed. They cannot speak for themselves. They are voiceless and at the mercy of calumny. No matter how grossly outraged, they must submit.

For a man clothed with the almost absolute power of a president to strike down men gagged and bound, as these men are, he must have an unspeakably brutal and cowardly nature, just such a nature as the governor of an empire state must have to turn a deaf ear to the agonizing entreaties of a shrieking, shuddering woman and see her dragged into the horrors of electrocution.

The true character of this man is being gradually revealed to the American people. He has never been anything but an enemy of the working class. He joined a labor organization purely as a demagogue. In all his life he never associated with working people. His writings, before he became a politician, show that he held them in contempt. When he entered political life he soon learned how to shake hands with a fireman for the camera and have his press agent do the rest, and it was this species of demagoguery, the very basest conceivable, that idolized him with the ignorant mass and gave him the votes of the millions he in his heart despised as an inferior race.

In his book on "Ranch Life and the Hunting Trail," page 10, written long before he entered politics, Roosevelt reveals his innate contempt for those who toil. After describing cowboys when "drunk on the villainous whiskey of the frontier towns," he closes with this comparison, which needs no comment: "They are much better fellows and pleasanter companions than small farmers or agricultural laborers; nor are the mechanics and workmen of a great city to be mentioned in the same breath."

The pretended friendship for the great body of workingmen who are not to be compared to drunken cowboys has served its demagogical purpose, but the final chapter is not yet written. There will be an awakening, and every official act of Theodore Roosevelt will be subjected to its searching scrutiny. He has always been on the side of capital wholly, while pretending the impossible feat of serving both capital and labor with equal fidelity, and only the deplorable ignorance of his dupes has applauded him in that hypocritical role.

The anthracite miners, or their children at least, will some day know that it was President Theodore Roosevelt who handed them over to the coal trust with a gold brick for a souvenir, labeled "Arbitration."

Theodore Roosevelt is an aristocrat and an autocrat. His affected democracy is spurious and easily detected. He belongs to the "upper crust" and at the very best he can conceive of the working class only as contented wage-slaves. And no one knows better than he how easily these slaves are duped and how madly they will cheer and follow a cheap and showy "hero."

The simple fact is that Theodore Roosevelt was made president by the industrial captains and the robbers in general of the working class. They picked him for a winner and he has not failed them. Elected by the trusts and surrounded by trust attorneys as cabinet advisers, Roosevelt is essentially the monarch of a trust administration.

If this be denied, Roosevelt is challenged to answer if it was not the railroad trust that furnished him gratuitously with the special trains that bore him in royal splendor over all the railways of the nation. He is challenged to publish the list of contributors to his political sewer funds, amounting to millions of dollars, and freely used to buy the votes that made him president.

Did, or did not, the men known as trust magnates put up this boodle? Boodle drawn from the veins of labor?

Will Mr. Roosevelt deny it?

Did he not know at the time that his man Cortelyou was holding up the trusts for all they would "cough up" for his election?

Will he dare plead ignorance to intelligent persons as to who put up the money that debauched the voters of the nation?

It is true that a spasm of virtuous indignation seized him when he found that the trusts had slipped the lucre into his slush funds when he was not looking, but this was only after he saw the people looking behind the curtain. Then he bounded to the foot-lights and denounced Alton B. Parker as a liar for charging that the trusts were furnishing the boodle to make him president, but no man not feeble-minded was deceived as to who was the liar.

Read the Washington press dispatch in the Kansas City *Journal* of April 4th: "It was declared in banking circles that light could be shed on the question of campaign contributions in 1904 if the books of the national Republican committee were thrown open."

The books will not be thrown open. Roosevelt will not allow it; he knows they contain the damning evidence of his guilt.

The case is clearly stated in the platform of the Democratic state convention of Missouri, adopted in 1906, which reads as follows:

"We believe Theodore Roosevelt insincere. Pretending to inveigh against the crimes of trusts and corporations, he openly defended Paul Morton, when, as manager of the Santa Fe railroad, he was compelled to confess enormous rebates to the Colorado Fuel and Iron Company. It was Roosevelt who advanced the pernicious doctrine that you must punish the corporation, not its officials who cause it to commit crime. It was Roosevelt who denounced large campaign contributions, while his secretary of commerce and labor was fleecing the corporations out of *one of the biggest slush funds ever known in the history of American politics."*

President Roosevelt may shout "liar" until he turns as black in the face as are the cracksmen at heart who burglarized the safes of the New York insurance companies to land him in the White House, while he was toying with the names of "Jimmy" Hyde and Chauncey Depew as pawns in the corrupt game, but the "damned spot" will not out until the whole truth is known and the whole crime expiated.

The publication of the Roosevelt-Harriman correspondence places the president in his true colors before the American people. It explains his hot haste in condemning Moyer, Haywood and Pettibone to the gallows and sending Taft to Idaho to assure the smelter trust and warn the protesting people that the kidnaping of the workingmen was sanctioned by the White House and would have the support of the national administration.

A more shameful perversion of public power never blackened the pages of history.

This national scandal shows up the president's two-faced character so clearly and convincingly that it leaves not so much as a pin-hole for escape. It is a damning indictment of not only the president, but the whole brood of plutocrats, promoters and grafting politicians who have been looting this nation for years.

There is one among these illuminating epistles which I want to burn in the minds of the working class dupes who have been bowing in the dust before this blustering bully of the White House:

"Personal.

"October 1, 1904.—My Dear Mr. Harriman: A suggestion has come to me in a round-about way that you do not think it wise to come to see me in these closing weeks of the campaign, but that you are reluctant to refuse, inasmuch as I have asked you. Now, my dear sir, you and I are practical men, and you are on the ground and know the conditions better than I do.

"If you think there is any danger of your visit to me causing trouble, or if you think there is nothing special I should be informed about, or any matter in which I could give aid, why, of course, give up the visit for the time being, and then, a few weeks hence, before I write my message, I shall get you to come down to discuss certain government matters not connected with the campaign. With great regards, sincerely yours,

(Signed) "THEODORE ROOSEVELT."

Does not this brand the president with the duplicity of a Tweed and the cunning of a Quay?

Would a president who is honest with the people clandestinely consort with the villain he characterizes as a liar and all that is vicious?

The disclosures made in the secret correspondence strip the president of the last shred of deception with which to cloak his perfidy. The mask is lifted and the exposure is complete. It is in the president's own handwriting in a letter to Harriman that would never have seen the light had not circumstances forced it upon the attention of a betrayed people. It is adroitly phrased, but its meaning is not in doubt. He knew Harriman then as he knows him now; wanted his boodle and insinuatingly coaxed him to sneak to the White House when no one was looking, and only after he was discovered did he denounce Harriman as a liar and fall into his usual fit of moral epilepsy.

From now on there will be a sharp decline in the stock of Theodore Roosevelt. The capitalist papers may continue to boom him as the only savior and his corps of press agents at the White House may continue to grind out three-column stories about the awful conspiracy of his "trusty" friends to ruin him, but his bubble is pricked and the cheap glory in which he reveled is departing forever.

The people have been sadly deceived for a time, but the march of events is opening their eyes.

Only the very ignorant and foolish believe that a president who has surrounded himself with Wall Street darlings as cabinet ministers has any serious designs on the trusts.

The Ryan, Root and Roosevelt combination is ideal. It speaks for itself, and with such shining lights as Taft, Cortelyou, Knox and Paul Morton surrounding it, all lingering doubt is removed, and the fools' paradise is in the full blaze of its glory.

Space will not permit a review of the personnel of the president's official family, at least two of whom, had the law been enforced, would now be in penitentiary.

The story of President Roosevelt and Paul Morton, if truthfully told, would make a luminous chapter in railroad rascality and political jobbery. It was to this notorious strike-breaker and self-confessed criminal that Roosevelt issued a bill of moral rectitude long as Pope's essay that landed him into the eighty-thousand-dollars-a-year insurance graft he now holds down.

There is in this "promotion" the very climax of the irony of boodle.

Paul Morton, who began as a strike-breaker on the C. B. & Q., and reared a monument to theft at Hutchinson, Kan., and left his trail of crime all the way from the Mississippi to the Pacific, is fit, indeed, to be the cabinet associate and confidential chum of a president who puts him at the head of the company whose funds were stolen to buy his election.

William H. Taft is another of the elect, and it is easy to understand why Roosevelt has decided to make this illustrious son his successor as president of the United States and is now grooming him with the patronage of the national administration. Taft is a man after Roosevelt's own heart. Among his early acts as a judge he fined the bricklayers of Cincinnati two thousand dollars for going on a strike; he was next whirled to Toledo by special train and ordered by the Toledo, Ann Arbor and North Michigan railroad to issue an injunction binding and gagging its striking engineers and firemen and locking their leader up in jail and he complied with alacrity. From that time on it has been smooth sailing for the accommodating judge and there is not a bloated plutocrat in the land who would not hail with joy the election of William Taft as president; he would be almost as acceptable to these vultures as Roosevelt himself.

The manner in which President Roosevelt manipulates the supreme court by bestowing lucrative offices upon the sons and other relatives and friends of its dignitaries can only be hinted at here, but will receive due attention later on. The case of ex-Senator Burton is an instance in point. Other senators had taken thousands in similar cases to Burton's paltry few hundred dollars, but Burton was marked by Roosevelt for refusing to crook the knee to the sugar trust and pursued with merciless ferocity until he was lodged behind prison bars.

The president did not have a call to "go after" his old friends, Chauncey Depew and Thomas Platt, with the same virtuous passion to see crime punished and criminals jailed.

When Roosevelt was making his continental campaign in the palatial special trains furnished free by the railroad trust he stopped at Abilene, Kan., the home of the then Senator Burton, and opened his speech there in these words: "I am glad to be at the home of the senior senator from Kansas and am delighted to meet and greet his neighbors and friends. I want to say that no man in this world has done more, and I had almost said, as much, to place me where I am now, than your distinguished senator."

Fine way the president had of showing his gratitude. Burton should have known better and taken warning. Whenever Roosevelt gets that near to a man something is going to happen. "My dear" is then due to be metamorphosed with startling suddenness into an "atrocious liar."

Roosevelt can brook no rivalry. He is the self-appointed central luminary in the solar system. All others must be contented with being fire-flies. He must violate all traditions and smash all precedents. He is spectacular beyond the wildest dreams. He must have the center of the stage and hold the undivided attention of the audience. Any stunt will do when the interest lags. A familiar turn with a prize-fighter or a "gun-man" is always good for an encore. Nothing is overlooked. A dash to Panama with a fleet of battle-ships and a battery of cameras and a squad of artists and reporters is good for thousands of columns about the marvelous virility and fertility of the greatest president since Washington. He is followed with minute and eager details as he darts from cellar to roof, inspects every shingle, wears a solemn expression, throws a shovelful of coal into the furnace, snatches a bite from a workingman's pail, shakes hands with a startled section man and is off like a flash to look after some other section of the planet that it may not drop out of its shining orbit.

Mighty savior of the human race!

Such is Theodore Roosevelt, the president who condemns workingmen as murderers when they are objectionable to the trusts that control his administration.

Archbishop Ireland, the plutocratic prelate, will cheerfully certify to Roosevelt as the anointed of the Lord. And this will make another interesting chapter for a later review; a chapter that will deal with Ireland as the political as well as spiritual adviser of "Jim" Hill and the Great Northern, and of court decisions awarding him thousands of acres of land and making of the alleged follower of the Tramp of Galilee a multi-millionaire; a chapter that will tell of a high priest sounding the political keynote to his benighted followers in exchange for a promised voucher for a red hat to be worn in a land of freedom in which the state and church are absolutely divorced.

Only a few of the facts about Roosevelt and his regime have been here stated, but enough to satisfy all honest men that *Theodore Roosevelt is the Friend of the Enemies and the Enemy of the Friends of this Republic.*

INDUSTRIAL AND SOCIAL DEMOCRACY. American Socialist, May 27, 1915.

First of all, allow me to quote with approval the following paragraph from "An Introduction to Sociology" by Arthur Morrow Lewis: " * * * the greatest single achievement of the science of sociology is the concept of society, not as a collection of institutions, and sociology as an explanatory catalog or inventory—after the fashion of Spencer, but as a process of development, and the science of sociology as the analysis and explanation of the process."

Also the following from an essay on Revolution by George D. Herron: "Every revolution or true reform, every new and commanding faith, is in the direction of man's becoming his own evolver and creator. Every uplifting light or law perforces, in the place of the evolution that is blind and chanceful, an evolution that is chosen and humanly directed."

There is still room for reform and betterment in the present social system, but this is of minor consequence compared to the world's crying need for industrial and social reorganization.

The next great change in history will be, must be, the socialization of the means of our common life.

Privately owned industry and production for individual profit are no longer compatible with social progress and have ceased to work out to humane and civilized ends.

With all its marvelous progress through invention and discovery and all its monumental achievements in the arts and sciences, this poor world of ours has not yet learned how to feed itself. That is the problem of problems now confronting us more and more insistently and until that is solved the world is halted and it will either resume its march toward industrial and social democracy or be shaken to its foundations and into possible chaos by violent explosion.

There is no longer the shadow of an excuse for a hungry being. All the laws, all the materials and all the forces are at hand and easily available for the production of all things needed to provide food, raiment and shelter for every man, woman and child, thus putting an end to the poverty and misery, widespread and appalling, which now shock and sicken humanity and impeach our vaunted civilization. But these tools and materials and forces must be released from private ownership and control, socialized, democratized, and set in operation for the common good of all instead of the private profit of the few.

It is well stated, "that civilization is at present rudimentary, and that it is to develop indefinitely."

Now, in view of the fact that the crops this year (1914) are the most abundant ever produced, that there is no market for the almost sixteen million bales of cotton lying in the warehouses, while at the same time there are millions of unemployed in the land who are without food and without clothing and who, with their wives and children, are doomed to indescribable suffering; in view of this solemn and indisputable fact it would seem that there could be but one opinion among students and thinkers as to the one great, vital and essential thing to do for the relief of our common humanity and for the promotion of the world's progress and civilization, and that that one thing is the one to be emphasized with all the power at our command.

A privately owned world can never be a free world and a society based upon warring classes cannot stand.

Such a world is a world of strife and hate and such a society can exist only by means of militarism and physical force.

The education of the people, not the few alone, but the entire mass in the principles of industrial democracy and along the lines of social development is the task of the people to be emphasized and that task—let it be impressed upon them—can be performed only by themselves.

The cultured few can never educate the uncultured many. All history attests the fact that all the few have ever done for the many is to keep them in ignorance and servitude and live out of their labor.

To stir the masses, to appeal to their higher, better selves, to set them thinking for themselves, and to hold ever before them the ideal of mutual kindness and good will, based upon mutual interests, is to render real service to the cause of humanity.

To quote Herron once more:

"Socialism is a deliberate proposal to lay the will of man upon the unfolding processes and ends of nature and history. It invokes the faith that shall be equal to the acceptance of its proposal—of its supreme challenge to the universe."

dec

A MESSAGE TO THE CHILDREN. Campaign Leaflet, National Campaign, 1912.

The Socialist party is the only party that has the children at heart; the only party that takes them into its confidence; the only party that has a message for them in a campaign year.

In my travels about the country I have met many thousands of little children and their fresh and eager faces have always given me joy and their merry voices have filled me with delight and made me stronger for my work.

These children are not yet old enough to join the Socialist party and have an active part in its great work, but they are old enough to understand why their parents belong to it, and why they are proud of their card of membership, and of the red button they wear, to show that they are socialists and that as socialists they are working hand in hand with thousands and thousands of others to change things so that this world may be a better, kinder and sweeter world for us all to live in.

Now let me talk directly as I may to the more than thirty millions of children and young folks in our country who are less than eighteen years of age. I fancy I can see them all spread out in all directions, far as the eye can reach, and farther and farther still to the very shores of the seas and lakes and gulf that bound our western continent.

What a wonderful audience I am about to address! Not a grown person in it. Only children. Millions of them and all eager to hear the message that socialism has to offer to the child-world.

My dear little children, I am sure you will understand me when I say that in speaking to you of socialism I feel very near to all of you and I know you will believe me when I tell you that I would if I could make you all happy and keep you sweet and loving toward each other all your lives. Most of you are the children of the poor, some of the well-to-do, and a few of the rich, but all of you are the children of the same Father and all of you are sisters and brothers in the same great family of humankind.

If any of you feel that you are better than others because you wear better clothes or live in better houses or go in what you think is "better society," it is because your young minds and hearts have been tainted by wrong example and wrong education. It is this wicked feeling that corrupts the conscience and hardens the heart and begets the envy and hate of our fellow-beings, instead of their love and good will.

When that best friend the children ever had on earth said, "Suffer little children and forbid them not, to come unto me; for such is the kingdom of heaven" he meant all children, poor and rich, but especially the poor. He loved and pitied them because of their poverty and suffering.

He himself had been born in a manger and when he was grown up he said sorrowfully that "he had not where to lay his head." He did not despise little children because they were poor and neglected and shabbily dressed but he loved them all the more; and as he looked down upon them his heart melted with compassion and the tears of tenderness filled his eyes; and then he became grave and his fair brow grew dark with wrath as he thought of those who sat in rich church pews and piously thanked the Lord that they were not as other people. He denounced them as hypocrites for pretending to be religious while they robbed the poor and turned the little children into the street to suffer hunger and fall into evil ways.

Nearly twenty centuries have passed since the suffering poor heard with gladness the message of the Lowly Nazarene and since he was moved to tears by the sight of the little children of the street, but the world has not yet learned the meaning of his tender and touching words, "Suffer little children, and forbid them not, to come unto me; for of such is the kingdom of heaven." If he were to walk the streets of New York or Chicago, or Lawrence, Massachusetts, or any of the cities where the mills and sweatshops are filled with child slaves—as he once walked the streets of Jerusalem—he would grow sick at heart as he saw the little ones he so loved, pale and wan and worn, harnessed to monstrous machines and slowly put to death to swell the profits of the greedy mill owners who sit in the rich pews of the synagogue, as did the pharisees he scourged without mercy twenty centuries ago.

The children of the working people have always been poor because the world has never been just. For ages and ages those who have builded the houses, cultivated the fields, raised the crops, spun the wool, woven the cloth, supplied the food we eat and the clothes we wear, and furnished the homes we live in, have been the poor and despised, while those who profited by their labor and consumed the good things they produced, have been the rich and respectable.

Jesus himself was a carpenter's son and suffered the poverty of his class and when he grew up it was not the rich and respectable, but the poor and despised who loved him, and opened their arms to receive him, and heard gladly his tender and comforting ministrations. He was one of them in poverty and suffering and in all his loving and self-denying life he never forgot them. Had he deserted the poor from whom he sprang, had he gone over to the rich as their preacher, or their judge, or their lawyer or teacher or scribe—as so many of his pretended followers have done and are still doing—he never would have been crucified, nor would the world today know that he had ever lived.

It was because, and only because, Jesus loved and served the poor and rebuked the rich who robbed them, and threatened to array them against their rich despoilers, that he was condemned to die and that the cruel nails were driven into his hands and feet on the cross at Calvary.

Jesus taught that the earth and the air and the sea and sky and all the beauty and fulness thereof were for all the children of men; that they should all equally enjoy the riches of nature and dwell together in peace, bear one another's burdens and love one another, and that is what socialism teaches and why the rich thieves who have laid hold of the earth and its bounties would crucify the socialists as those other robbers of the poor crucified Jesus two thousand years ago.

Now let us see what message the Socialist party has for the children and why all children should be socialists and help to speed the day when the brotherhood of socialism shall prevail throughout the earth.

But first let me say that the Socialist party has reason to know that the children have great influence when they become interested in a given work and set their hearts on doing that work. The Socialist party knows better than to ignore the children as if they were china dolls or stuffed teddy bears, as all the other parties do, for it knows by what they have already done that when once they get fairly started they will make the air hum like swarms of bees with the glad tidings of socialism.

The little boys and girls who have already become socialists are among the busiest workers for our party and they love so well to work for socialism that it is play to them and fills their hearts with joy. They wear the red button and they know why it is red and what its meaning is; they tack up bills and distribute dodgers advertising our meetings; they sell tickets, take up collections, act as ushers, provide the soap-box for the corner speaker, carry chairs for the women so they may sit in comfort after their day's work, go around among the neighbors and remind them of the meeting and not to forget to attend, sell socialist books, papers and pamphlets, and do a score of other things which are just as useful in their way as the speech of the orator that wins the applause of the people.

Now the Socialist party is the only party in the world that wants to put an end once and forever to all kinds of child labor and to have it so that all children, white and black, without a single exception, shall be allowed to grow up in the free air, with plenty of time for mirth and play; that they shall all have decent homes to live in, comfortable beds to sleep in, plenty of good food to eat, plenty of good clothes to wear and that when they reach the proper age they shall go to school and college and continue their course until they have obtained a sound and practical education. Then they will have strong, healthy bodies, trained minds and skilled hands, and not only enter cheerfully upon the duties of life, but be certain of making it a success.

If you listen to the old fogies who still belong to the parties their grandfathers did and who have not moved an inch from their grandfathers' graves, they will tell you that socialists are foolish people and that what they propose never can be done. That is what the fogies of every age have always said. They are the "wise" people who do things in the same way that their dead grandparents did before them, who never change their minds, never accept a new idea, never grow, and who are always dead long before they are buried and forgotten the day after the funeral. Whatever you may be I beg of you not to be a fogy, nor to follow a fogy's solemn advice. His brain has ceased to work—if it ever did work. He is mentally stagnant and moss-covered and votes the same old ticket with no more idea of what he is voting for than a wooden Indian.

The Socialist party says there have got to be some changes and has set about making them, or at least getting ready to make them. It says that the world is big enough for all the people that are in it, with plenty of room to spare for groves and parks and playgrounds; that there is land enough to go

56

around without crowding; that there are farms enough, or can be easily provided, to raise all we can eat, so that no child in all the world need to go hungry; that there is plenty of coal and iron, oil and gas, gold and silver and other minerals and metals, stored in the earth; that there are forests and mountains and water courses galore; that there are mills and mines and factories and ships and railways and telegraphs, and the power supplied free by nature to run them all; that there are millions of men and women ready to do all the work that may be required to build homes, raise crops, bake bread—and cake too—weave cloth, make clothes and everything else that is necessary for everybody, and have time enough besides to build schools and provide playgrounds for every last one of the children, with plenty of toys thrown in to make this earth a children's paradise.

Now why should not just these things come to pass and why should not you children help us speed the day when they *shall* come to pass?

Everything you can possibly think of to make this earth sweet and beautiful and to make life a blessed joy for us all is within our reach. The raw materials are at our feet; the forces to fashion them into forms of beauty and use are at our finger tips. We have but to put ourselves in harmony with nature and with one another to spread far and wide the gospel of life and love and once more hear "the sons of God shout for joy."

Socialists not only dream of the good day coming when the world shall know that men are brothers and that women are sisters to each other, but they are at work with all their hearts and all their heads and hands to make that dream come true.

If you want to know what the plans of the socialists are in detail read their platform, attend their lectures and study their literature.

Socialism is the greatest thing in all the world today and the boys and girls of this generation who will be remembered in the next are those who are clear-eyed enough to see that socialism is coming and are at the battle-front fighting bravely to overcome the prejudice against it and to pave the way for it so that it may come soon and in peace and order.

Many of us who have been long in service will not be here when the bells peal forth the joyous tidings that socialism has triumphed and that the people are free, but the children that now are will live to see it and in the day of their rejoicing they will not forget those who toiled without recompense that they might live without dread of poverty or fear of want.

As we look about us today we see that the world is filled with suffering and despair and when we come to look into the cause of it we find that it is a reproach to us all. As I write the news comes of the fierce battle that is being fought between ten thousand hungry miners in West Virginia and the thugs and ex-convicts and murderers armed by the coal corporations to force the strikers back into their dismal and hopeless pits. The battle has already lasted two days. Many on both sides have been killed, but the capitalist papers are doing all they can to hush it up.

Long ago the miners were evicted from the company's wretched hovels. They and their wives and children live in tented fields and the brutal guards have even driven the women and children from there into the wilderness to starve that the strike may be broken and the miners compelled to go back to work at the terms of their greedy and heartless masters.

And why is this awful battle raging and human beings murdering each other as if they were wild beasts? Because a few gluttonous slave owners like Henry Gassaway Davis and the Watsons and Elkinses who dwell in gorgeous palaces on vast estates occupying whole mountain ranges, privately own the mines and minerals which were intended for all, and consequently the thousands of miners and their wives and children are at their mercy, and when they meekly asked for five per cent more wages so their families would not suffer for bread the brutal lords of the mines sent out their private army of assassins to hunt them down and kill them as if they were mad dogs.

The Socialist party says that those mines should be owned by all the people and that is what will come to pass when the socialists get into power, and then the green hills of West Virginia and other states will no longer echo with the rifle shots of corporation assassins, nor run red with the blood of honest workingmen slain to appease the greed of their soulless masters.

In February last, four boys were hanged in Chicago. The oldest was twenty-one, the youngest barely out of his childhood. They had held up and robbed and murdered a poor truck farmer for the little money he had on his person. Not one of these boys ever had a decent home. They were born in poverty, reared in ignorance, and surrounded by vice and filth.

This is cultivating crime and reaping the harvest. We socialists weep as we think of the cruel fate of those four poor, friendless boys who died on the gallows while they were still in their childhood, because the world has not yet learned that there is greater profit in raising children than there is in raising hogs.

The frightful stories of the little children in the mills of Lawrence and the cruel suffering they endured is still fresh in the public memory. When the poor and despairing mothers, their hearts wrung with agony and their eyes blinded with tears, attempted to save their children from starvation by placing them in the keeping of sympathizing friends, they were beaten, insulted, and with babies at their breasts thrown into jail, bleeding and stunned, by the brutal police acting under orders from the far more brutal mill owners.

The world will never know the suffering and terror these poor working people—especially the women and children—had to endure for daring to ask the millionaire mill owners for a pittance more in return for their labor to keep the wolf of hunger from their gloomy hovels.

When the Socialist party gets into power those mills at Lawrence and all others like them will be taken over by the people and operated for the good of all, and then the workers will keep the wealth they produce for themselves, instead of turning it over to the greedy mill bosses; they will have decent homes to live in, food in plenty on their tables, and their children will go to school to be properly educated instead of to the mills to be ground into profits to gorge their idle owners.

In March last, Mrs. L. F. Jellson of Salem, Oregon, gave poison to each of her four little children, her own offspring, because they were starving and she was poor and had no way to get them bread. She then poisoned herself and all she asked in the note she left was that she and her darling children be buried together. This poor heart-broken soul was driven to destroy herself and her precious babes because the world as it now is would not allow them to live.

Think for just a moment of all the food there is in the world and all there might be and then tell me if socialists are wrong and foolish and wicked for saying that the self-murder of this poor woman and the murder of her children is a terrible crime of which society is guilty and for which there is no excuse on earth or in heaven.

A recent investigation showed that in the City of St. Louis there are

16,000 young women who receive as wage-earners less than $8 per week and over 3,000 who receive from $3 to $4 per week.

It is easy to see from this why so many little girls and younger women are forced to enter upon the path which leads to shame and sorrow and which seldom bears the impress of returning footsteps.

When the giant Titanic met her fate, fifty little bellboys went down with her to the bottom of the sea. They were ordered, according to the account, to their regular posts in the main cabin and warned by their captain not to get into the way of the escaping passengers. James Humphries, as quartermaster and eye witness said, "throughout the first hour of confusion and terror these lads sat quietly on their benches. Not one of them attempted to enter a lifeboat. Not one of them was saved."

Can you read this without being moved to tears? Brave, noble little lads! I almost feel as if it had been a privilege to go down with these great little souls to their watery grave.

The little boys who perished here were poor boys, many of them without fathers, and others obliged to support widowed mothers and little brothers and sisters younger than themselves.

What a lesson this touching, deeply pathetic incident teaches and what a world of meaning there is in the sad circumstances of their tragic death!

Had they not been poor children, little waifs, they would not have been locked in the cabin to perish like rats. They would not, in fact, have been there at all, and had it not been for the pride and pomp, the greed and luxury that paraded the upper deck, the Titanic never would have gone to the bottom of the sea.

And now, my children, I must come to a close. I have taken up much of your time, but I have only been able to trace in barest outline what the Socialist party is organized for, what it aims to do, and will do, and why the children, above all, should vie with each other in helping it to grow and speeding the happy day of its success.

When that day comes the rejoicing people will realize that the kingdom of heaven, so long prayed for, has been set up here on earth in the social brotherhood of all mankind.

dec

SOCIAL REFORM.

While there is a lower class I am in it; While there is a criminal class I am of it; While there is a soul in prison I am not free.

dec

DANGER AHEAD. International Socialist Review, January, 1911.

The large increase in the Socialist vote in the late national and state elections is quite naturally hailed with elation and rejoicing by party members, but I feel prompted to remark, in the light of some personal observations made during the campaign, that it is not entirely a matter of jubilation. I am not given to pessimism, or captious criticism, and yet I cannot but feel that some of the votes placed to our credit this year were obtained by methods not consistent with the principles of a revolutionary party, and in the long run will do more harm than good.

I yield to no one in my desire to see the party grow and the vote increase, but in my zeal I do not lose sight of the fact that healthy growth and a substantial vote depend upon efficient organization, the self-education and self-discipline of the membership, and that where these are lacking, an inflated vote secured by compromising methods, can only be hurtful to the movement.

The danger I see ahead is that the Socialist party at this stage, and under existing conditions, is apt to attract elements which it cannot assimilate, and that it may be either weighted down, or torn asunder with internal strife, or that it may become permeated and corrupted with the spirit of bourgeois reform to an extent that will practically destroy its virility and efficiency as a revolutionary organization.

To my mind the working class character and the revolutionary integrity of the Socialist party are of first importance. All the votes of the people would do us no good if our party ceased to be a revolutionary party, or came to be only incidentally so, while yielding more and more to the pressure to modify the principles and program of the party for the sake of swelling the vote and hastening the day of its expected triumph.

It is precisely this policy and the alluring promise it holds out to new members with more zeal than knowledge of working class economics, that constitutes the danger we should guard against in preparing for the next campaign. The truth is that we have not a few members who regard vote-getting as of supreme importance, no matter by what method the votes may be secured, and this leads them to hold out inducements and make representations which are not at all compatible with the stern and uncompromising principles of a revolutionary party. They seek to make the Socialist propaganda so attractive—eliminating whatever may give offense to bourgeois sensibilities—that it serves as a bait for votes rather than as a means of education, and votes thus secured do not properly belong to us and do injustice to our party as well as to those who cast them.

These votes do not express socialism and in the next ensuing election are quite as apt to be turned against us, and it is better that they be not cast for the Socialist party, registering a degree of progress the party is not entitled to and indicating a political position the party is unable to sustain.

Socialism is a matter of growth, of evolution, which can be advanced by wise methods, but never by obtaining for it a fictitious vote. We should seek only to register the actual vote of socialism, no more and no less. In our propaganda we should state our principles clearly, speak the truth fearlessly, seeking neither to flatter nor to offend, but only to convince those who should be with us and win them to our cause through an intelligent understanding of its mission.

There is also a disposition on the part of some to join hands with reactionary trade-unionists in local emergencies and in certain temporary situations to effect some specific purpose, which may or may not be in harmony with our revolutionary program. No possible good can come from any kind of a political alliance, express or implied, with trade-unions or the leaders of trade unions who are opposed to socialism and only turn to it for use in some extremity, the fruit of their own reactionary policy.

Of course we want the support of trade-unionists, but only of those who believe in socialism and are ready to vote and work with us for the overthrow of capitalism.

The American Federation of Labor, as an organization, with its Civic federation to determine its attitude and control its course, is deadly hostile to the Socialist party and to any and every revolutionary movement of the working class. To kowtow to this organization and to join hands with its leaders to secure political favors can only result in compromising our principles and bringing disaster to the party.

Not for all the vote of the American Federation of Labor and its labor-dividing and corruption breeding craft-unions should we compromise one jot of our revolutionary principles; and if we do we shall be visited with the contempt we deserve by all real Socialists, who will scorn to remain in a party professing to be a revolutionary party of the working class while employing the crooked and disreputable methods of ward-heeling politicians to attain their ends.

Of far greater importance than increasing the vote of the Socialist party is the economic organization of the working class. To the extent, and only to the extent, that the workers are organized and disciplined in their respective industries can the Socialist movement advance and the Socialist party hold what is registered by the ballot. The election of legislative and administrative officers, here and there, where the party is still in a crude state and the members economically and politically unfit to assume the responsibilities thrust upon them as the result of popular discontent, will inevitably bring trouble and set the party back, instead of advancing it, and while this is to be expected and is to an extent unavoidable, we should court no more of that kind of experience than is necessary to avoid a repetition of it. The Socialist party has already achieved some victories of this kind which proved to be defeats, crushing and humiliating, and from which the party has not even now, after many years, entirely recovered.

We have just so much socialism that is stable and dependable, because securely grounded in economics, in discipline and all else that expresses class-conscious solidarity, and this must be augmented steadily through economic and political organization, but no amount of mere votes can accomplish this in even the slightest degree.

A vote for socialism is not socialism any more than a menu is a meal.

Socialism must be organized, drilled, equipped, and the place to begin is in the industries where the workers are employed. Their economic power has got to be developed through efficient organization, or their political

63

power, even if it could be developed, would but react upon them, thwart their plans, blast their hopes, and all but destroy them.

Such organization to be effective must be expressed in terms of industrial unionism. Each industry must be organized in its entirety, embracing all the workers, and all working together in the interests of all, in the true spirit of solidarity, thus laying the foundation and developing the superstructure of the new system within the old, from which it is evolving, and systematically fitting the workers, step by step, to assume entire control of the productive forces when the hour strikes for the impending organic change.

Without such economic organization and the economic power with which it is clothed, and without the industrial co-operative training, discipline and efficiency which are its corollaries, the fruit of any political victories the workers may achieve will turn to ashes on their lips.

Now that the capitalist system is so palpably breaking down, and in consequence its political parties breaking up, the disintegrating elements with vague reform ideas and radical bourgeois tendencies will head in increasing numbers toward the Socialist party, especially since the greatly enlarged vote of this year has been announced and the party is looming up as a possible dispenser of the spoils of office. There is danger, I believe, that the party may be swamped by such an exodus and the best possible means—and, in fact, the only effectual means—of securing the party against such a fatality is the economic power of the industrially-organized workers.

The votes will come rapidly enough from now on without seeking them and we should make it clear that the Socialist party wants the votes only of those who want socialism, and that, above all, as a revolutionary party of the working class, it discountenances vote-seeking for the sake of votes and holds in contempt office-seeking for the sake of office. These belong entirely to capitalist parties with their bosses and their boodle and have no place in a party whose shibboleth is emancipation.

With the workers efficiently organized industrially, bound together by the common tie of their enlightened self-interest, they will just as naturally and inevitably express their economic solidarity in political terms and cast a united vote for the party of their class as the forces of nature express obedience to the law of gravitation.

dec
PIONEER WOMEN IN AMERICA. Progressive Woman, April, 1912.

In looking over some old letters a day or two ago I found a postal card which Susan B. Anthony had written to me over thirty years ago, and, strangely enough, it was held fast by a letter that was written to me about the same time by Wendell Phillips, as if these two epistles had been attracted to each other and held together in the bonds of mutualism as were the great souls who had written them in their heroic struggle for human enfranchisement.

The faded and time-worn old card carried me back to the day I met Miss Anthony at the depot on her arrival at Terre Haute, where she was to speak in public for her sex. At that time Mrs. Ida Husted Harper, who afterward became Miss Anthony's confidential friend and authorized biographer, and I, and two or three others, were about the only people in Terre Haute who believed that woman was a human being and entitled to the rights of citizenship. We had arranged these meetings for Miss Anthony and her three active coadjutors in woman's cause at that time, and they arrived according to the schedule.

I shall never forget how Miss Anthony impressed me. She had all the charm of a real woman and all the strength of a perfect man. Style, personal adornment, she did not know; vanity found no lodgment in her great soul. She was born with a heroic purpose, and she set out in fulfillment of that purpose with a spirit of dauntless valor and determination which knew "no variableness or shadow of turning" to the day that ended her consecrated life and she passed from the scenes of men.

The trials, privations, insults borne by this grand old pioneer will never be known by those who are in the ranks today. An event characteristic of the struggle in which she engaged almost single-handed for so many years was her arrest and trial for voting in the presidential election of 1872. A fine of one hundred dollars and costs was imposed upon her, which she vowed she would not pay, even if she were sent to jail. When Miss Anthony said a thing she meant it. That fine was never paid.

It was, after all, a stroke of good fortune that Miss Anthony was the victim of this barbarous indignity. It inspired one of the greatest speeches of her life. In opening this dramatic plea and protest she said:

"Friends and Fellow-Citizens: I stand before you tonight under indictment for the alleged crime of having voted at the last presidential election, without having a lawful right to vote. It shall be my work this evening to prove to you that in thus voting I not only committed no crime, but, instead, simply exercised my citizen's rights, guaranteed to me and all United States citizens by the National Constitution, beyond the power of any State to deny."

She then quoted from the preamble of the Federal Constitution: "We, the *people* of the United States," etc., and proceeded:

"It was we, the people; not we, the white male citizens; nor yet we the male citizens; but, we the whole people, who formed the union. And we formed it, not to give the blessings of liberty, but to secure them; not to the half of ourselves and the half of our posterity, but to the whole people—women as well as men. And it is a downright mockery to talk to women of their enjoyment of the blessings of liberty while they are denied the use of the only means of securing them provided by this democratic-republican government—the ballot. The early journals of Congress show that when the committee reported to that body the original articles of confederation, the very first article which became the subject of discussion was that respecting equality of suffrage. Article 4 said: 'The better to secure and perpetuate mutual friendship and intercourse between the people of the different States of the Union, the free inhabitants of each of the States (paupers, vagabonds and fugitives from justice excepted) shall be entitled to all the privileges and immunities of the free citizen, of the several States.'

"Thus, at the very beginning did the fathers see the necessity of the universal application of the great principle of equal rights to all, in order to produce the desired results—a harmonious union and a homogeneous people."

Miss Anthony then quoted the New York State Constitution: "No member of this State shall be disfranchised or deprived of the rights or privileges secured to any citizen thereof, unless by the law of the land or the judgment of its peers."

She then proceeded with her argument, which has never been and never will be answered. It is to be regretted that space forbids more ample quotation in this article. Here is a glowing paragraph from her impassioned plea which is characteristic of the entire address:

"To them (women) this government has no just powers derived from the consent of the governed. To them this government is not a democracy. It is not a republic. It is an odious aristocracy; a hateful oligarchy of sex; the most hateful aristocracy ever established on the face of the globe; an oligarchy of wealth, where the rich govern the poor. An oligarchy of learning, where the educated govern the ignorant, or even an oligarchy of race, where the Saxon rules the African, might be endured; but this oligarchy of sex, which makes father, brothers, husband, sons the oligarch over the mother and sisters, the wife and daughters of every household; which ordains all men sovereigns, all women subjects; carries dissension, discord and rebellion into every home of the nation."

There has never been a more logical unanswerable argument for the political enfranchisement of women than was here made by Miss Anthony. And yet only a very few of the people were fair enough to listen, intelligent enough to understand, or candid enough to give approval, if they did.

Susan B. Anthony's whole career was one tempestuous struggle for the rights of her sex. She never wavered and she never wearied in the conflict. She had the moral courage of a martyr, and such she was as certainly as any that ever perished at the stake.

On my visit to Johnstown, N. Y., recently, the comrades pointed out the spot where Elizabeth Cady Stanton, another pioneer heroine of the movement, was born. Mrs. Stanton has long since been gathered to her fathers, but her work remains an imperishable monument in memory of her achievements.

It was at the first Woman's Rights convention ever held in the United States, July 19, 1848, that Mrs. Stanton delivered an oration that will forever have a place in the literature of woman's struggle for freedom. The doctrine she advocated was at that time little less than treason, but she knew it was *true*, and she boldly took her stand and maintained it to the end. In her speech at this first convention she said:

"Now is the time for the women of this country, if they would save our free institutions, to defend the right, to buckle on the armor that can best resist the keenest weapons of the enemy—contempt and ridicule. The same religious enthusiasm that nerved Joan of Arc to her work nerves us to ours. In every generation God calls some men and women for the utterance of the truth, a heroic action, and our work today is the fulfilling of what has long since been foretold by the prophet. * * * We do not expect our path will be strewn with the flowers of popular applause, but over the thorns of bigotry and prejudice will be our way, and on our banner will beat dark storm-clouds of opposition from those who have entrenched themselves behind the stormy bulwarks of custom and authority, and who have fortified their position by every means, holy and unholy. But we will steadfastly abide the result. Unmoved we will bear it aloft. Undauntedly we will unfurl it to the gale, for we know that the storm cannot rend from it a shred, that the electric flash will but more clearly show to us the glorious words inscribed upon it: 'Equality of Rights.'"

There was thrilling power in the burning eloquence of Mrs. Stanton, but only they who had a part in the struggle at that time could have any conception of what bitter hatred, blind prejudice and malign persecution there were to overcome.

In February, 1854, Mrs. Stanton made a notable plea for the political rights of women to the legislature of New York. In mentally invoicing an average legislature today one gets some idea of the self-imposed task of this brave old pioneer, and the indomitable spirit required to undertake it, of arousing a body of sodden bourgeois legislators, ward politicians, to recognize the right of women to breathe the air of civilized citizenship and belong to themselves. In this thoroughly militant and inspiring appeal she said:

"The tyrant, Custom, has been summoned before the bar of Common Sense. His majesty no longer awes the multitude; his scepter is broken; his crown is trampled in the dust; the sentence of death is pronounced upon him. All nations, ranks and classes have, in turn, questioned and repudiated his authority; and now, that the monster is chained and caged, timid woman, on tiptoe, comes to look him in the face, and to demand of her brave sires and sons, who have struck stout blows for liberty, if, in this change of dynasty, she, too, shall find relief. * * *

"We demand the full recognition of all our rights as citizens of the Empire State. We are persons; natives, free-born citizens; property holders, taxpayers, yet we are denied the exercise of our right to the elective franchise. We support ourselves, and, in part, your schools, colleges, churches, your poor-houses, jails, prisons, the army, the navy, the whole machinery of government, and yet we have no voice in your councils. We have every qualification required by the constitution necessary to the legal voter but the one of sex. We are moral, virtuous and intelligent, and in all respects quite equal to the proud white man himself, and yet by your laws we are classed with idiots, lunatics and negroes."

These two sturdy pioneers in woman's struggle present a magnificent picture in the perspective. They did not know the meaning of discouragement. They were strangers to weakness and fear.

Both were of heroic mould. Both were born and endowed for great service and both made their names synonymous with the struggle of their sex to shake off the fetters of the centuries.

Mrs. Stanton was born in 1815, ante-dating Miss Anthony by five years. They were inseparable friends, and they who saw them together say that their love and fealty toward each other was so beautiful and touching that it was an inspiration to all their co-workers and shamed to silence all their bickerings and petty jealousies.

They both lived to be over eighty years. After full half a century of unrelaxing fidelity to their principles and unceasing battle for their cause they saw but the beginning of the glorious fruition of their consecrated service. Such has been the fate of all who, like these great souls, loved principle better than popularity and humanity more than themselves.

The women who are in the ranks today may well rejoice that these grand women and others who shared in their bitter persecution blazed the way through the dense wilderness of ignorance, prejudice and hatred for what is now a world movement, with millions proudly bearing its banner, inscribed with the conquering shibboleth: Equal Freedom and Equal Opportunities for All Mankind.

SPEECHES

UNITY AND VICTORY. Speech Before State Convention of American Federation of
Labor, Pittsburg, Kansas, August 12, 1908.

Introduction by Chairman Cable.

Gentlemen of the Convention: I assure you it is a great privilege on my part to present to you at this time a gentleman who needs no introduction at my hands; a gentleman who is known to you and who is known to the workingmen throughout the length and breadth of this country as a true and tried trade unionist and the candidate of the Socialist party for President of the United States. I, therefore, take great pleasure in presenting to you Brother Eugene V. Debs.

Mr. Chairman, Delegates and Fellow Workers: It is with pleasure, I assure you, that I embrace this opportunity to exchange greetings with you in the councils of labor. I have prepared no formal address, nor is any necessary at this time. You have met here as the representatives of organized labor and if I can do anything to assist you in the work you have been delegated to do I shall render that assistance with great pleasure.

To serve the working class is to me always a duty of love. Thirty-three years ago I first became a member of a trade union. I can remember quite well under what difficulties meetings were held and with what contempt organized labor was treated at that time. There has been a decided change. The small and insignificant trade union has expanded to the proportions of a great national organization. The few hundreds now number millions and organized labor has become a recognized factor in the economics and politics of the nation.

There has been a great evolution during that time and while the power of the organized workers has increased there has been an industrial development which makes that power more necessary than ever before in all the history of the working class movement.

This is an age of organization. The small employer of a quarter of a century ago has practically disappeared. The workingman of today is confronted by the great corporation which has its ironclad rules and regulations, and if they don't suit he can quit.

In the presence of this great power, workingmen are compelled to organize or be ground to atoms. They have organized. They have the numbers. They have had some bitter experience. They have suffered beyond the power of language to describe, but they have not yet developed their latent power to a degree that they can cope successfully with the great power that exploits and oppresses them. Upon this question of organization, my brothers, you and I may differ widely, but as we are reasonable men, we can discuss these differences candidly until we find common ground upon which we can stand side by side in the true spirit of solidarity—and work together for the emancipation of our class.

Until quite recently the average trade unionist was opposed to having politics even mentioned in the meeting of his union. The reason for this is self-evident. Workingmen have not until now keenly felt the necessity for independent working class political action. They have been divided between the two capitalist parties and the very suggestion that the union was to be used in the interest of the one or the other was in itself sufficient to sow the seed of disruption. So it isn't strange that the average trade unionist guarded carefully against the introduction of political questions in his union. But within the past two or three years there have been such changes that workingmen have been compelled to take notice of the fact that the labor question is essentially a political question, and that if they would protect themselves against the greed and rapacity of the capitalist class they must develop their political power as well as their economic power, and use both in their own interest. Workingmen have developed sufficient intelligence to understand the necessity for unity upon the economic field. All now recognize the need for thorough organization. But organization of numbers of itself is not sufficient. You might have all the workers of the country embraced in some vast organization and yet they would be very weak if they were not organized upon correct principles; if they did not understand, and understand clearly, what they were organized for, and what their organization expected to accomplish.

I am of those who believe that an organization of workingmen, to be efficient, to meet the demands of this hour, must be organized upon a revolutionary basis; must have for its definite object not only the betterment of the condition of workingmen in the wage system, but the absolute overthrow of wage slavery that the workingman may be emancipated and stand forth clothed with the dignity and all other attributes of true manhood.

Now let me briefly discuss the existing condition. We have been organizing all these years, and there are now approximately three millions of American workingmen who wear union badges, who keep step to union progress. At this very time, and in spite of all that organized labor can do to the contrary, there is a condition that prevails all over this country that is well calculated to challenge the serious consideration of every workingman. To begin with, according to the reports furnished us, twenty per cent of the workingmen of this country are now out of employment. I have here a copy of the New York World containing a report of the labor commissioner of the State of New York who shows that during the quarter ending June 30 there were in that state an army of union men out of employment approximating thirty-five per cent of the entire number; that is to say, in the State of New York today, out of every one hundred union men (these reports are received from the unions themselves, verified by their own officers, so there can be no question in regard to them), out of every 100 union men in New York, 35 are out of employment. The percentage may not be so large in these western states where the industrial development has not reached the same point, but go where you may, east or west, north or south, you will find men, union men, who are begging for the opportunity to work for just enough to keep their suffering souls within their famished bodies. A system in which such a condition as this is possible has fulfilled its mission, stands condemned, and ought to be abolished.

According to the Declaration of Independence, man has the inalienable right to life. If that be true it follows that he has also the inalienable right to work.

If you have no right to work you have no right to life because you can

72

only live by work. And if you live in a system that deprives you of the right to work, that system denies you the right to live. Now man has a right to life because he is here. That is sufficient proof, and if he has the right to life, it follows that he has the right to all the means that sustain life. But how is it in this outgrown capitalist system? A workingman can only work on condition that he finds somebody who will give him permission to work for just enough of what his labor produces to keep him in working order.

No matter whether you have studied this economic question or not, you cannot have failed to observe that during the past half century society has been sharply divided into classes—into a capitalist class upon the one hand, into a working class upon the other hand. I shall not take the time to trace this evolution. I shall simply call your attention to the fact that half a century ago all a man needed was a trade and having this he could supply himself with the simple tools then used, produce what he needed and enjoy the fruit of his labor. But this has been completely changed. The simple tool has disappeared and the great machine has taken its place. The little shop is gone and the great factory has come in its stead. The worker can no longer work by and for himself. He has been recruited into regiments, battalions and armies and work has been subdivided and specialized; and now hundreds and thousands and tens of thousands of workingmen work together co-operatively and produce in great abundance, not for themselves, however, for they no longer own the tools they work with. What they produce belongs to the capitalist class who own the tools with which they work. A man fifty years ago who made a shoe owned it. Today it is possible for that same worker, if still alive, to make a hundred times as many shoes, but he doesn't own them now. He works today with modern machinery which is the property of some capitalist who lives perhaps a thousand miles from where the factory is located and who owns all the product because he owns the machinery.

I have stated that society has been divided into two warring classes. The capitalist owns the tool in modern industry, but he has nothing to do with its operation. By virtue of such ownership he has the economic power to appropriate to himself the wealth produced by the use of that tool. This accounts for the fact that the capitalist becomes rich. But how about the working class? In the first place they have to compete with each other for the privilege of operating the capitalist's tool of production. The bigger the tool and the more generally it is applied, the more it produces, the sharper competition grows between the workers for the privilege of using it and the more are thrown out of employment. Every few years, no matter what party is in power, no matter what our domestic policy is, how high the tariff or what the money standard, every few years the cry goes up about "over-production" and the working class is discharged by the thousands and thousands, and are idle, just as the miners have been in this field for many weary months.

No work, no food, and after a while, no credit, and all this in the shadow of the abundance these very workers have created.

Don't you agree with me, my brothers, that this condition is an intolerable and indefensible one, and that whatever may be said of the past, this system no longer answers the demands of this time? Why should any workingman need to beg for work? Why forced to surrender to anybody any part of what his labor produces?

Now, I ask this question, and it applies to the whole field of industry: If a hundred men work in a mine and produce a hundred tons of coal, how much of that coal are they entitled to? Are they not entitled to all of it? And if not, who is entitled to any part of it? If the man who produces wealth is not entitled to it, who is? You say the capitalist is necessary and I deny it. The capitalist has become a profit-taking parasite. Industry is now concentrated and operated on a very large scale; it is co-operative and therefore self-operative. The capitalists hire superintendents, managers and workingmen to operate their plants and produce wealth. The capitalists are absolutely unnecessary; they have no part in the process of production—not the slightest.

Now I insist that it is the workingman's duty to so organize economically and politically as to put an end to this system; as to take possession in his collective capacity of the machinery of production and operate it, not to create millionaires and multi-millionaires, but to produce wealth in plenty for all. That is why the labor question is also a political question. It makes no difference what you do on the economic field to better your condition, so long as the tools of production are privately owned, so long as they are operated for the private profit of the capitalist, the working class will be exploited, they will be in enforced idleness, thousands of them will be reduced to want, some of them to vagabonds and criminals, and this condition will prevail in spite of anything that organized labor can do to the contrary.

The most important thing for the workingman to recognize is the class struggle. Every capitalist, every capitalist newspaper, every capitalist attorney and retainer will insist that we have no classes in this country and that there is no class struggle. President Roosevelt himself has declared that class-consciousness is a foul and evil thing. Now, what is class-consciousness? It is simply a recognition of the fact on the part of the workingman that his interest is identical with the interest of every other workingman. Class-consciousness points out the necessity for working-class action, economic and political.

What is it that keeps the working class in subjection? What is it that is responsible for their exploitation and for all of the ills they suffer? Just one thing; it can be stated in a single word. It is *Ignorance*. The working class have not yet learned how to unite and act together. There are relatively but few capitalists in this country; there are perhaps twenty millions of wage workers, but the capitalists and their retainers have contrived during all these years to keep the working class divided, and as long as the working class is divided it will be helpless. It is only when the working class learn—and they are learning daily and by very bitter experience—to unite and to act together, especially on election day, that there is any hope for emancipation.

The workingmen you represent, my brothers, are in an overwhelming majority in every township, county and state of this nation. You declare you are in favor of united action, but still you don't unite. You unite under certain conditions within your union, you get together upon the economic field to a limited extent, but you have yet to learn that before you can really accomplish anything you have got to unite in fact as well as in name. The time is coming when workingmen will be forced into one general organization. The time is coming when they will be compelled to organize on the basis of industrial unionism.

At this very hour there is a strike on the Canadian Pacific. Eight thousand workingmen who are more or less organized and who have been wronged in many ways, have finally gone out on strike. There are other thousands remaining at their posts and non-union men flowing in there will be hauled to their destination by union men, and union men will continue to work until their eight thousand brothers have lost their jobs and many of them have become tramps. That is called organization, but it is not so in fact. It is at best organization of a very weak and defective character. Now, the right kind of organization on the Canadian Pacific would embrace all the workers. They should all be included within the same organization and then have one general working agreement with the company so that if there was a violation of it, it would concern every man in the service. But how is it at present? The engineers, conductors, trainmen and switchmen are in separate unions and after they have been signed up, the company can treat the rest just as they please, for they know that if they strike and the others remain in their service, as they are bound to do under their agreement, they can very easily supplant them and remain in perfect control of the system. We have had enough of that kind of experience and we ought to profit by it. We ought to realize that there is but one form of organization that answers completely, one in which all subscribe to the same rules and act together in all things, and you will have to organize upon that basis or see your unions become practically worthless.

Now let us consider another line briefly for the benefit of those who have opposed political action. We are all aware of the trend of the decisions recently rendered by the United States supreme court. Three decisions have been rendered in rapid succession which strike down the rights of labor and virtually strip organized labor of its power. Under these decisions organized labor has been outlawed, and while upon this question I want to suggest that this body at the proper time in its deliberations put the following questions to the candidates for the United States senate and house of representatives in the State of Kansas and request them to answer:

In view of the fact that the United States supreme court has rendered a number of decisions placing the working class at a tremendous disadvantage in its struggle with the employing class for better conditions, we respectfully submit to the candidates for the United States senate and house of representatives the following questions:

1. Are you in favor of issuing injunctions against trade union members because they refuse to patronize a non-union employer and advise

their friends to do likewise?

2. Will you introduce and vote for a measure setting aside the decision of the supreme court of the District of Columbia in the case of Buck Stove and Range Company against officers of the A. F. of L., making it a criminal act for a labor union to place an employer on its unfair list?

3. Are you in favor of classifying trade unions as "trusts in restraint of trade," as was done by the supreme court in the case of Lowe vs. Lawler, and will you introduce a measure, should you be elected, providing for the exemption of trade unions from the operation of the anti-trust law under this court decision?

4. Do you endorse the supreme court decision making it lawful for a corporation to discharge a man because of his membership in a labor union? If you do not, will you introduce and vote for a bill setting aside this decision of the supreme court and making it unlawful for a corporation to discharge a man because he is a member of a trade union?

Here are these candidates in the State of Kansas for the United States senate and house of representatives and if they are elected they will have the power to control legislation, and it is perfectly proper that you, as the representatives of the workers, should put these questions squarely to these candidates and demand that they answer them. They are very simple questions. The United States court has rendered a decision to the effect that a trade union is a trust and that if it exercises its legitimate powers it is a criminal conspiracy in restraint of trade. That decision of the court congress has the power to set aside, and if a man stands as a candidate for congress, in the upper or lower branch, and appeals to you for your vote—and bear in mind he can only be elected by your vote—it is right and proper that you should know if he is in favor of the decision or opposed to it. And if he is in favor of this decision he is your enemy.

Now, these candidates are trying to carry water on both shoulders. They declare they will give both labor and capital a square deal, and I want to say that is impossible. No man can be for labor without being against capital. No man can be for capital without being against labor.

Here is the capitalist; here are the workers. Here is the capitalist who owns the mines; here are the miners who work in the mines. There is so much coal produced. There is a quarrel between them over a division of the product. Each wants all he can get. Here we have the class struggle. Now, is it possible to be for the capitalist without being against the worker? Are their interest not diametrically opposite?

If you increase the share of the capitalist don't you decrease the share of the workers? Can a door be both open and shut at the same time? Can you increase both the workers' and the capitalist's share at the same time? There is just so much produced, and in the present system it has to be divided between the capitalists and the workers, and both sides are fighting for all they can get, and this is the historic class struggle.

We have now no revolutionary organization of the workers along the lines of this class struggle, and that is the demand of this time. The pure and simple trade union will no longer answer. I would not take from it the least credit that belongs to it. I have fought under its banner for thirty years. I have followed it through victory and defeat, generally defeat. I realize today more than ever before in my life the necessity for thorough economic organization. It must be made complete. Organization, like everything else, is subject to the laws of evolution. Everything changes, my brothers. The tool you worked with twenty-five years ago will no longer do. It would do then; it will not do now. The capitalists are combined against you. They are reducing wages. They have control of the courts. They are doing everything they can to destroy your power. You have got to follow their example. You have got to unify your forces. You have got to stand together shoulder to shoulder on the economic and political fields and then you will make substantial progress toward emancipation.

I am not here, my brothers, to ask you, as an economic organization, to go into politics. Not at all. If I could have you pass a resolution to go into politics I would not do it. If you were inclined to go into active politics as an organization I would prevent such action if I could. You represent the economic organization of the working class and this organization has its own clearly defined functions. Your economic organization can never become a political machine, but your economic organization must recognize and proclaim the necessity for a united political party. You ought to pass a resolution recognizing the class struggle, declaring your opposition to the capitalist system of private ownership of the means of production, and urging upon the working class the necessity for working class political action. That is as far as the economic organization need to go. If you were to use your economic organization for political purposes you would disrupt it, you would wreck it.

But I would not have you renounce politics, nor be afraid to discuss anything. Who is it that is so fearful you will discuss politics? It is the ward-heeling politician, and isn't it because he knows very well that if you ever get into politics in the right way he will be out of a job? He is afraid you will get your eyes open.

Why should a union man be afraid to discuss politics? He belongs to a certain party; his father belonged to that party and his grandfather belonged to that party, and perhaps his great-grandfather belonged to the same party, and that is probably the only reason he can give for belonging to that party. He don't want anybody to suggest to him the possibility of being lifted out of that party and into some other.

Parties change. The party that was good forty years ago is completely outgrown and corrupt and has now no purpose but the promotion of graft and other vicious practices.

Workingmen in their organized capacity must recognize the necessity for both economic and political action. I would not have you declare in favor of any particular political party. That would be another mistake which would have disastrous results. If I could have you pass a resolution to support the Socialist party I would not do it. You can't make Socialists by passing resolutions. Men have to become Socialists by study and experience, and they are getting the experience every day.

There is one fact, and a very important one, that I would impress upon you, and that is the necessity for revolutionary working class political action.

No one will attempt to dispute the fact that our interests as workers are identical. If our interests are identical, then we ought to unite. We ought to unite within the same organization, and if there is a strike we should all strike, and if there is a boycott all of us ought to engage in it. If our interests are identical, it follows that we ought to belong to the same party as well as to the same economic organization. What is politics? It is simply the reflex of economics. What is a party? It is the expression politically of certain material

79

class interests. You belong to that party that you believe will promote your material welfare. Is not that a fact? If you find yourself in a party that attacks your pocket do you not quit that party?

Now, if you are in a party that opposes your interests it is because you don't have intelligence enough to understand your interests. That is where the capitalists have the better of you. As a rule, they are intelligent, and shrewd. They understand their material interests and how to protect them. You find the capitalists as a rule belonging only to capitalist parties. They don't join a working-class party and they don't vote the Socialist ticket. They know enough to know that Socialism is opposed to their economic interests. Now, both republican and democratic parties are capitalist parties. There is not the slightest doubt about it. It can be proved in a hundred different ways. You know how the republican party treated the demands of labor in its recent national convention. You know, or ought to know, what has taken place under the present administration. You know, or ought to know, something about the democratic party, national, state and municipal. If there are those who say that the democratic party is more favorable to labor than the republican party it is only necessary to point to the southern states where it has ruled for a century. In no other part of the nation are workingmen in so wretched a condition. In no other part are working people so miserably housed, so wretchedly treated as they are in the southern states where the democratic party rules supreme.

At this very hour miners in Alabama are on strike under a democratic administration. I know the condition there, for I have been in the mines. I know many of those men personally. I know under what conditions they have had to work. I have been in the shacks in which they live and have seen their unhappy wives and ill-fed children. I know whereof I speak. Only in the last extremity have those men gone out on strike. They bore all these cruel wrongs for years and were finally forced out on strike. And then what happened? The very first thing the democratic governor did was to send the soldiers to scab the mines. It doesn't make any difference to you, if workingmen are starved and shot down, which party is in power. It occurs under both republican and democratic administration. There will be no change as long as you continue to support the prevailing capitalist system, based upon the private ownership of the tools with which workingmen work

80

and without which they are doomed to slavery and starvation.

Now, I repeat that this body should declare against this system of private ownership and in favor of the collective ownership by the workers of the tools of production. This will give you a clear aim and definite object. This will make your movement revolutionary in its ultimate purpose, as it ought to be, and as for immediate concessions in the way of legislation by capitalist representatives and more favorable working conditions, you workingmen have only to poll two million Socialist votes this fall, and you will get those concessions freely and you will not get them in any other way. You will not frighten, you will not move the great corporations by dividing your votes between the republican and democratic parties. It doesn't make any difference which of these two parties wins, you lose! They are both capitalist parties and I don't ask you to take my mere word for it. I simply ask, my brothers, that you read and study the platforms for yourself. I beg of you not to have an ignorant, superstitious reverence for any political party. It is your misfortune if you are the blind follower of any political leader, or any other leader. It is your duty as a workingman, your duty to yourself, your family, to quit a party the very instant you find that that party no longer serves you; and if you continue to adhere to a party that antagonizes your interests, if you continue to support a system in which you are degraded, then you have no right to complain. You must submit to what comes, for you yourself are responsible.

Let me impress this fact upon your minds: the labor question, which is really the question of all humanity, will never be solved until it is solved by the working class. It will never be solved for you by the capitalists. It will never be solved for you by the politicians. It will remain unsolved until you yourselves solve it. As long as you can stand and are willing to stand these conditions, these conditions will remain; but when you unite all over the land, when you present a solid class-conscious phalanx, economically and politically, there is no power on this earth that can stand between you and complete emancipation.

As individuals you are helpless, but united you represent an irresistible power.

Is there any doubt in the mind of any thinking workingman that we are in the midst of a class struggle? Is there any doubt that the workingman ought to own the tool he works with? You will never own the tool you work with under the present system. This whole system is based upon the private ownership by the capitalist of the tools and the wage-slavery of the working class, and as long as the tools are privately owned by the capitalists the great mass of workers will be wage-slaves.

You may, at times, temporarily better your condition within certain limitations, but you will still remain wage-slaves, and why wage-slaves? For just one reason and no other—you have got to work. To work you have got to have tools, and if you have no tools you have to beg for work, and if you have got to beg for work the man who owns the tools you use will determine the conditions under which you shall work. As long as he owns your tools he owns your job, and if he owns your job he is the master of your fate. You are in no sense a free man. You are subject to his interest and to his will. He decides whether you shall work or not. Therefore, he decides whether you shall live or die. And in that humiliating position any one who tries to persuade you that you are a free man is guilty of insulting your intelligence. You will never be free, you will never stand erect in your own manly self-reliance until you are the master of the tools you work with, and when you are you can freely work without the consent of any master, and when you do work you will get all your labor produces.

As it is now the lion's share goes to the capitalist for which he does nothing, while you get a small fraction to feed, clothe and shelter yourself, and reproduce yourself in the form of labor power. That is all you get out of it and all you ever will get in the capitalist system.

Oh, my brothers, can you be satisfied with your lot? Will you insist that life shall continue a mere struggle for existence and one prolonged misery to which death comes as a blessed relief?

How is it with the average workingman today? I am not referring to the few who have been favored and who have fared better than the great mass, but I am asking how it is with the average workingman in this system? Admit that he has a job. What assurance has he that it is his in twenty-four hours? I have a letter from an expert glass worker saying that the new glass machine which has recently been tested, has proven conclusively that bottles can be made without a glass blower. Five or six boys with these machines can make as many bottles as ten expert blowers could make. Machinery is conquering every department of activity. It is displacing more and more workingmen and making the lot of those who have employment more and more insecure. Admit that a man has a job. What assurance has he that he is going to keep it? A machine may be invented. He may offend the boss. He may engage in a little agitation in the interest of his class. He is marked as an agitator, he is discharged, and then what is his status?

The minute he is discharged he has to hunt for a new buyer for his labor power. He owns no tools; the tools are great machines. He can't compete against them with his bare hands. He has got to work. There is only one condition under which he can work and that is when he sells his labor power, his energy, his very life currents, and thus disposes of himself in daily installments. He is not sold from the block, as was the chattel slave. He sells ten hours of himself every day in exchange for just enough to keep himself in that same slavish condition.

The machine he works with has to be oiled, and he has to be fed, and the oil sustains the same relation to the machine that food does to him. If he could work without food his wage would be reduced to the vanishing point. That is the status of the workingman today.

What can the present economic organization do to improve the condition of the workingman? Very little, if anything. If you have a wife and two or three children, and you take the possibilities into consideration, this question ought to give you grave concern. You know that it is the sons of workingmen who become vagabonds and tramps, and who are sent to jail, and it is the daughters of workingmen who are forced into houses of shame.

You are a workingman, you live in capitalism, and you have nothing but your labor power, and you don't know whether you are going to find a buyer or not. But even if you do find a master, if you have a job, can you boast of being a man among men?

No man can rightly claim to be a man unless he is free. There is something godlike about manhood. Manhood doesn't admit of ownership. Manhood scorns to be regarded as property.

Do you know whether you have a job or not? Do you know how long you are going to have one? And when you are out of a job what can your union do for you? I was down at Coalgate, Oklahoma, on the Fourth of July last, where six hundred miners have been out of work for four long months. They are all organized. There are the mines and machinery, and the miners are eager to work. But not a tap of work is being done, and the miners and their families are suffering, and most of them live in houses that are unfit for habitation. This awful condition is never going to be changed in capitalism. There is one way only and that is to wipe out capitalism, and to do that we have to get together, and when we do that we will find the way to emancipation.

You may not agree with me now, but make note of what I am saying. The time is near when you will be forced into economic and political solidarity.

The republican and democratic parties are alike capitalist parties. Some of you may think that Mr. Bryan, if elected, will do great things for the workers. Conditions will remain substantially the same. We will still be under capitalism. It will not matter how you may tinker with the tariff or the currency. The tools are still the property of the capitalists and you are still at their mercy.

Now let me show you that Mr. Bryan is no more your friend than is Mr. Taft. You remember when the officials of the Western Federation of Miners were kidnaped in Colorado, and when it was said they should never leave Idaho alive. It was the determination of the Mine Owners' Association that these brave and loyal union leaders should be foully murdered. When these brothers of ours were brutally kidnaped by the collusion of the capitalist governors of two states, every true friend of the working class cried out in protest. Did Mr. Bryan utter a word? Mr. Bryan was the recognized champion of the working class. He was in a position to be heard. A protest from him would have tremendous weight with the American people. But his labor friends could not unlock his lips. Not one word would he speak. Not one.

Organized labor, however, throughout the length and breadth of the land, took the matter in hand promptly and registered its protest in a way that made the nation quake. The Mine Owners' Association took to the tall timber. Our brother unionists were acquitted, vindicated, and stood forth without a blemish upon their honor, and after they were free once more, Mr. Bryan said, "I felt all the time that they were not guilty."

Now if your faithful leaders are kidnaped and threatened to be hanged, and you call upon a man who claims to be your friend, to come to the rescue and he refuses to say a word, to give the least help, do you still think he is your friend? Mr. Bryan had his chance to prove his friendship at a time when labor sorely needed friends, when organized labor cried out in agony and distress. But not a word escaped his lips.

Why did not Mr. Byran speak? He did not dare. Mr. Bryan knew very well that the kidnapers of those men were his personal friends, the association of rich mine owners, who had largely furnished his campaign funds. For Mr. Bryan personally I have always had a high regard. I am not attacking him in any personal sense at all.

But the extremity to which a man is driven who tries to serve both capital and labor! It can't be done. Mr. Bryan did not dare to speak for labor because if he had he would have turned the mine owning capitalists against him. He is afraid to speak out very loudly for capitalists for fear the workers will get after him. He has compromised all around for the sake of being president.

You have heard him denounce Roger Sullivan. Mr. Bryan, four years ago, in denouncing this corruptionist, at the time of the nomination of Alton B. Parker, said he was totally destitute of honor and compared him to a train robber. Notwithstanding this fact, Mr. Bryan recently invited Sullivan to his home in Lincoln, took him by the hand and introduced him to his family. Mr. Bryan also invited Charley Murphy, the inexpressibly rotten Tammany heeler of New York. Mr. Bryan had him come to Lincoln so as to conciliate Tammany, and they were photographed together shaking hands.

No man can serve both capital and labor at the same time.

You don't admit the capitalists to your union. They organize their union to fight you. You organize your union to fight them. Their union consists wholly of capitalists; your union consists wholly of workingmen. It is along the same line that you have got to organize politically. You don't unite with capitalists on the economic field; why should you politically?

You have got to extend your class line. You can declare yourselves in this convention and make your position clear to the world. You can give hope and inspire confidence throughout the state.

And now in closing, I wish to thank you, each of you, from my heart, for your kindness. I appreciate the opportunity you have given me to address you and whether you agree with me or not, I leave you wishing you success in your deliberations and hoping for the early triumph of the labor movement.

The convention passed a unanimous rising vote of thanks at the close of the address.

dec

POLITICAL APPEAL TO AMERICAN WORKERS. Opening Speech of National Campaign, Riverview Park, Chicago, June 16, 1912.

Friends, Comrades and Fellow-Workers: We are today entering upon a national campaign of the profoundest interest to the working class and the country. In this campaign there are but two parties and but one issue. There is no longer even the pretense of difference between the so-called Republican and Democratic parties. They are substantially one in what they stand for. They are opposed to each other on no question of principle but purely in a contest for the spoils of office.

To the workers of the country these two parties in name are one in fact. They, or rather, it, stands for capitalism, for the private ownership of the means of subsistence, for the exploitation of the workers, and for wage-slavery.

Both of these old capitalist class machines are going to pieces. Having outlived their time they have become corrupt and worse than useless and now present a spectacle of political degeneracy never before witnessed in this or any other country. Both are torn by dissension and rife with disintegration. The evolution of the forces underlying them is tearing them from their foundations and sweeping them to inevitable destruction.

We have before us in this city at this hour an exhibition of capitalist machine politics which lays bare the true inwardness of the situation in the capitalist camp. Nothing that any Socialist has ever charged in the way of corruption is to be compared with what Taft and Roosevelt have charged and proven upon one another. They are both good Republicans, just as Harmon and Bryan are both good Democrats—and they are all agreed that Socialism would be the ruination of the country.

Puppets of the Ruling Class.

Taft and Roosevelt in the exploitation of their boasted individualism and their mad fight for official spoils have been forced to expose the whole game of capitalist class politics and reveal themselves and the whole brood of capitalist politicians in their true role before the American people. They are all the mere puppets of the ruling class. They are literally bought, paid for and owned, body and soul, by the powers that are exploiting this nation and enslaving and robbing its toilers.

What difference is there, judged by what they stand for, between Taft, Roosevelt, La Follette, Harmon, Wilson, Clark and Bryan?

Do they not all alike stand for the private ownership of industry and the wage-slavery of the working class?

What earthly difference can it make to the millions of workers whether the Republican or Democratic political machine of capitalism is in commission?

That these two parties differ in name only and are one in fact is demonstrated beyond cavil whenever and wherever the Socialist party constitutes a menace to their misrule. Milwaukee is a case in point and there are many others. Confronted by the Socialists these long pretended foes are forced to drop their masks and fly into each other's arms.

Twin Agencies of Wall Street.

The baseness, hypocrisy and corruption of these twin political agencies of Wall Street and the ruling class cannot be expressed in words. The imagination is taxed in contemplating their crimes. There is no depth of dishonor to which they have not descended—no depth of depravity they have not sounded.

To the extent that they control elections the franchise is corrupted and the electorate debauched, and when they succeed in power it is but to execute the will of the Wall Street interests which finance and control them. The police, the militia, the regular army, the courts and all the powers lodged in class government are all freely at the service of the ruling class, especially in suppressing discontent among the slaves of the factories, mills and mines, and keeping them safely in subjugation to their masters.

How can any intelligent, self-respecting wage-worker give his support to either of these corrupt capitalist parties? The emblem of a capitalist party on a working man is the badge of his ignorance, his servility and shame.

Marshalled in battle array, against these corrupt capitalist parties is the young, virile, revolutionary Socialist party, the party of the awakening working class, whose red banners, inscribed with the inspiring shibboleth of class-conscious solidarity, proclaim the coming triumph of international Socialism and the emancipation of the workers of the world.

The Two Political Forces.

Contrast these two political forces and the parties through which these forces find concrete expression! On the one side are the trusts, the corporations, the banks, the railroads, the plutocrats, the politicians, the bribe-givers, the ballot-box stuffers, the repeaters, the parasites, retainers and job-hunters of all descriptions; the corruption funds, the filth, slime and debauchery of ruling class politics; the press and pulpit and college, all wearing capitalism's collar, and all in concert applauding its "patriotism" and glorifying in its plundering and profligate regime.

On the other side are the workers and producers of the nation coming into consciousness of their interests and their power as a class, filled with the spirit of solidarity and thrilled with the new-born power that throbs within them; scorning further affiliation with the parties that so long used them to their own degradation and looking trustfully to themselves and to each other for relief from oppression and for emancipation from the power which has so long enslaved them.

Honest toil, useful labor, against industrial robbery and political rottenness!

These are the two forces which are arrayed against each other in deadly and uncompromising hostility in the present campaign.

Corrupt Capitalist Politics.

We are not here to play the filthy game of capitalist politics. There is the same relative difference between capitalist class politics and working class politics that there is between capitalism and Socialism.

Capitalism, having its foundation in the slavery and exploitation of the masses, can only rule by corrupt means and its politics are essentially the reflex of its low and debasing economic character.

The Socialist party as the party of the working class stands squarely upon its principles in making its appeal to the workers of the nation. It is not begging for votes, nor seeking for votes, nor bargaining for votes. It is not in the vote market. It wants votes, but only of those who want it—those who recognize it as their party and come to it of their own free will.

If, as the Socialist candidate for president, I were seeking office and the spoils of office I would be a traitor to the Socialist party and a disgrace to the working class.

To be sure we want all the votes we can get and all that are coming to us but only as a means of developing the political power of the working class in the struggle for industrial freedom, and not that we may revel in the spoils of office.

Political Power.

The workers have never yet developed or made use of their political power. They have played the game of their masters for the benefit of the master class—and now many of them, disgusted with their own blind and stupid performance, are renouncing politics and refusing to see any difference between the capitalist parties financed by the ruling class to perpetuate class rule and the Socialist party organized and financed by the workers themselves as a means of wresting the control of government and of industry from the capitalists and making the working class the ruling class of the nation and the world.

The Socialist party enters this campaign under conditions that could scarcely be more favorable to the cause it represents. For the first time every state in the union is now organized and represented in the national party, and every state will have a full ticket in the field; and for the first time the Socialists of the United States have a party which takes its rightful place in the great revolutionary working class movement of the world.

Four years ago with a membership of scarcely forty thousand we succeeded in polling nearly half a million votes; this year when the campaign is fairly opened we shall have a hundred and fifty thousand dues-paying members and an organization in all regards incalculably superior to that we had in the last campaign.

We are united, militant, aggressive, enthusiastic as never before. From the Eastern coast to the Pacific shore and from the Canadian line to the Mexican gulf the red banner of the proletarian revolution floats unchallenged and the exultant shouts of the advancing hosts of labor are borne on all the breezes.

There Is But One Issue.

There is but one issue that appeals to this conquering army—the unconditional surrender of the capitalist class. To be sure this cannot be achieved in a day and in the meantime the party enforces to the extent of its power its immediate demands and presses steadily onward toward the goal. It has its constructive program by means of which it develops its power and its capacity, step by step, seizing upon every bit of vantage to advance and strengthen its position, but never for a moment mistaking reform for revolution and never losing sight of the ultimate goal.

Socialist reform must not be confounded with so-called capitalist reform. The latter is shrewdly designed to buttress capitalism; the former to overthrow it. Socialist reform vitalizes and promotes the social revolution.

The National Convention.

The national convention of the Socialist party recently held at Indianapolis was in all respects the greatest gathering of representative Socialists ever held in the United States. The delegates there assembled demonstrated their ability to deal efficiently with all the vital problems which confront the party. The convention was permeated in every fiber with the class-conscious, revolutionary spirit and was thoroughly representative of the working class. Every question that came before that body was considered and disposed of in accordance with the principles and program of the international movement and on the basis of its relation to and effect upon the working class.

The platform adopted by the convention is a clear and cogent enunciation of the party's principles and a frank and forceful statement of the party's mission. This platform embodies labor's indictment of the capitalist system and demands the abolition of that system. It proclaims the identity of interests of all workers and appeals to them in clarion tones to unite for their emancipation. It points out the class struggle and emphasizes the need of the economic and political unity of the workers to wage that struggle to a successful issue. It declares relentless war upon the entire capitalist regime in the name of the rising working class and demands in uncompromising terms the overthrow of wage-slavery and the inauguration of industrial democracy.

In this platform of the Socialist party the historic development of society is clearly stated and the fact made manifest that the time has come for the workers of the world to shake off their oppressors and exploiters, put an end to their age-long servitude, and make themselves the masters of the world.

To this end the Socialist party has been organized; to this end it is bending all its energies and taxing all its resources; to this end it makes its appeal to the workers and their sympathizers throughout the nation.

The Capitalist System Condemned.

In the name of the workers the Socialist party condemns the capitalist system. In the name of freedom it condemns wage-slavery. In the name of modern industry it condemns poverty, idleness and famine. In the name of peace it condemns war. In the name of civilization it condemns the murder of little children. In the name of enlightenment it condemns ignorance and superstition. In the name of the future it arraigns the past at the bar of the present, and in the name of humanity it demands social justice for every man, woman and child.

The Socialist party knows neither color, creed, sex, nor race. It knows no aliens among the oppressed and down-trodden. It is first and last the party of the workers, regardless of their nationality, proclaiming their interests, voicing their aspirations, and fighting their battles.

It matters not where the slaves of the earth lift their bowed bodies from the dust and seek to shake off their fetters, or lighten the burden that oppresses them, the Socialist party is pledged to encourage and support them to the full extent of its power. It matters not to what union they belong, or if they belong to any union, the Socialist party which sprang from their struggle, their oppression, and their aspiration, is with them through good and evil report, in trial and defeat, until at last victory is inscribed upon their banner.

Fighting Labor's Battles.

Whether it be in the textile mills of Lawrence and other mills of New England where men, women and children are ground into dividends to gorge a heartless, mill-owning plutocracy; or whether it be in the lumber and railroad camps of the far Northwest where men are herded like cattle and insulted, beaten and deported for peaceably asserting the legal right to organize; or in the conflict with the civilized savages of San Diego where men who dare be known as members of the Industrial Workers of the World are kidnaped, tortured and murdered in cold blood in the name of law and order; or in the city of Chicago where that gorgon of capitalism, the newspaper trust, is bent upon crushing and exterminating the pressmen's union; or along the Harriman lines of railroad where the slaves of the shops have been driven to the alternative of striking or sacrificing the last vestige of their manhood and self-respect, in all these battles of the workers against their capitalist oppressors the Socialist party has the most vital concern and is freely pledged to render them all the assistance in its power.

These are the battles of the workers in the war of the classes and the battles of the workers, wherever and however fought, are always and everywhere the battles of the Socialist party.

When Moyer, Haywood and Pettibone were seized by the brutal mine owners of the western states and by their prostitute press consigned to the gallows, the Socialist party lost not an hour in going to the rescue, and but for its prompt and vigorous action and the resolute work of its press another monstrous crime against the working class would have blackened the pages of American history.

Persecution of Loyal Leaders.

In the unceasing struggle of the workers with their exploiters the truly loyal leaders are always marked for persecution. Joseph Ettor and Arturo Giovannitti would not now be in jail awaiting trial for murder had they betrayed the slaves of the Lawrence mills. They were staunch and true; their leadership made for industrial unity and victory, and for this reason alone the enraged and defeated mill-owners are now bent upon sending them to the electric chair.

These fellow-workers of ours who are now on trial for murder are not one whit more guilty of the crime with which they are charged than I am. The man who committed the murder was a policeman, an officer of the law; the victim of the crime was as usual a striker, a wage-slave, a poor working girl. Ettor and Giovannitti were two miles from the scene at the time and when the news came to them they broke into tears—and these two workingmen who would have protected that poor girl's life with their own are now to be tried for her murder.

Was ever anything in all the annals of heartless persecution more monstrous than this? Have the mill-owners gone stark mad? Have they in their brutal rage become stone-blind? Whatever the answer may be, it is certain that the Socialist party and organized labor in general will never see these two innocent workers murdered in cold blood, nor will their agitation and protest cease until they have been given their freedom.

The Campaign Now Opening.

In the great campaign now pending the people, especially the toilers and producers, will be far more receptive to the truths of Socialism than ever before.

Since the last national campaign they have had four years more of capitalism, of political corruption, industrial stagnation, low wages and high prices, and many, very many of them have come to realize that these conditions are inherent in the capitalist system and that it is vain and foolish to hope for relief through the political parties of that system. These people have had their eyes opened in spite of themselves. They have been made to see what the present system means to them and to their children, and they have been forced to turn against it by the sheer instinct of self-preservation.

They look abroad and they see this fair land being rapidly converted into the private preserves of a plutocracy as brutal and defiant as any privileged class that ever ruled in a foreign despotism; they see machinery and misery go hand in hand; they see thousands idle and poverty-stricken all about them while a few are glutted to degeneracy; they see troops of child-slaves ground into luxuries for the rich while their fathers have become a drug on the labor market; they see parasites in palaces and automobiles and honest workers in hovels or tramping the ties; they see the politics of the ruling corporations dripping with corruption and putridity; they see vice and crime rampant, prostitution eating like a cancer, and insanity and disease sapping the mental and physical powers of the body social, and involuntarily they cry out in horror and protest, THIS IS ENOUGH! THERE MUST BE A CHANGE! And they turn with loathing and disgust from the Republican and Democratic parties under whose joint and several maladministration these appalling conditions have been brought upon the country.

The message of Socialism, which a few years ago was spurned by these people, falls today upon eager ears and receptive minds. Their prejudice has melted away. They are now prepared to cast their fortunes with the only political party that proposes a change of system and the only party that has a right to appeal to the intelligence of the people.

First Socialist Congressman.

The political beginning of the Socialist party in this country is now distinctly recognized by its most implacable enemies. A single Socialist congressman has been sufficient to arouse the whole nation to the vital issue of Socialism which confronts it. Victor L. Berger as the first and until now the only representative of labor, has had the power, single-handed and alone, to compel the respectful consideration of the American congress, for the first time in its history, of the rights and interests of the working class. To be sure the capitalists do not relish this and so they have consolidated the Republican and Democratic forces in Berger's district to defeat him, but the rising tide of Socialism will overwhelm them both and not only triumphantly re-elect Berger but a score of others to make the next congress resound with the demands of the working class.

Now is the time for the workers of this nation to develop and assert their political as well as their economic power, to demonstrate their unity and solidarity.

Back up the economic victory at Lawrence with an overwhelming victory at the ballot box! Sweep the minions of the mill-owners from power and fill every office from the ranks of the workers! Deliver a crushing rebuke to the hireling-officials of San Diego by a united vote of the workers that will rescue the city from the rule of the degenerates and place it forever under a working class administration.

The Only Democratic Party.

The Socialist party is the only party of the people, the only party opposed to the rule of the plutocracy, the only truly democratic party in the world.

It is the only party in which women have equal rights with men, the only party which denies membership to a man who refuses to recognize woman as his political equal, the only party that is pledged to strike the fetters of economic and political slavery from womanhood and pave the way for a race of free women.

The Socialist party is the only party that stands a living protest against the monstrous crime of child labor. It is the only party whose triumph will sound once and forever the knell of child slavery.

There is no hope under the present decaying system. The worker who votes the Republican or Democratic ticket does worse than throw his vote away. He is a deserter of his class and his own worst enemy, though he may be in blissful ignorance of the fact that he is false to himself and his fellow-workers and that sooner or later he must reap what he has sown.

Wages and Cost of Living.

The latest census reports, covering the year 1909, show that the 6,615,046 workers in manufactories in the United States were paid an average wage of $519 for the year, an increase of not quite 9 per cent in five years, and an increase of 21 per cent in ten years, but the average cost of living increased more than 40 per cent during the same time, so that in point of fact the wages of these workers have been and are being steadily reduced in the progressive development of production under the capitalist system, and this in spite of all the resistance that has been or can be brought to bear by the federated craft unions. Here we are brought face to face with the imperative need of the revolutionary industrial union, embracing all the workers and fighting every battle for increased wages, shorter hours and better conditions with a solid and united front, while at the same time pressing steadily forward in harmonious co-operation and under the restraints of self-discipline, developing the latent abilities of the workers, increasing their knowledge, and fitting them for the mastery and control of industry when the victorious hosts of labor conquer the public powers and transfer the title-deeds of the mines and mills and factories from the idle plutocrats to the industrial workers to be operated for the common good.

Industrial Unity.

If the printing trades were organized on the basis of industrial unionism the spectacle of local unions in the same crafts pitted against each other to their mutual destruction would not be presented to us in the City of Chicago, and the capitalist newspaper trust would not now have its heel upon the neck of the union pressmen. For this lamentable state of affairs the craft union and William Randolph Hearst, its chief patron and promoter, are entirely responsible.

The Socialist party presents the farm workers as well as the industrial workers with a platform and program which must appeal to their intelligence and command their support. It points out to them clearly why their situation is hopeless under capitalism, how they are robbed and exploited, and why they are bound to make common cause with the industrial workers in the mills and factories of the cities, along the railways and in the mines in the struggle for emancipation.

The education, organization and co-operation of the workers, the entire body of them, is the conscious aim and the self-imposed task of the Socialist party. Persistently, unceasingly and enthusiastically this great work is being accomplished. It is the working class coming into consciousness of itself, and no power on earth can prevail against it in the hour of its complete awakening.

Socialism Is Inevitable.

The laws of evolution have decreed the downfall of the capitalist system. The handwriting is upon the wall in letters of fire. The trusts are transforming industry and next will come the transformation of the trusts by the people. Socialism is inevitable. Capitalism is breaking down and the new order evolving from it is clearly the Socialist commonwealth.

The present evolution can only culminate in industrial and social democracy, and in alliance therewith and preparing the way for the peaceable reception of the new order, is the Socialist movement, arousing the workers and educating and fitting them to take possession of their own when at last the struggle of the centuries has been crowned with triumph.

In the coming social order, based upon the social ownership of the means of life and the production of wealth for the use of all instead of the private profit of the few, for which the Socialist party stands in this and every other campaign, peace will prevail and plenty for all will abound in the land. The brute struggle for existence will have ended, and the millions of exploited poor will be rescued from the skeleton clutches of poverty and famine. Prostitution and the white slave traffic, fostered and protected under the old order, will be a horror of the past.

The social conscience and the social spirit will prevail. Society will have a new birth, and the race a new destiny. There will be work for all, leisure for all, and the joys of life for all.

Competition there will be, not in the struggle for existence, but to excel in good work and in social service. Every child will then have an equal chance to grow up in health and vigor of body and mind and an equal chance to rise to its full stature and achieve success in life.

Socialist Ideals.

These are the ideals of the Socialist party and to these ideals it has consecrated all its energies and all its powers. The members of the Socialist party *are* the party and their collective will is the supreme law. The Socialist party is organized and ruled from the bottom up. There is no boss and there never can be unless the party deserts its principles and ceases to be a Socialist party.

The party is supported by a dues-paying membership. It is the only political party that is so supported. Each member has not only an equal voice but is urged to take an active part in all the party councils. Each local meeting place is an educational center. The party relies wholly upon the power of education, knowledge, and mutual understanding. It buys no votes and it makes no canvass in the red-light districts.

The press of the party is the most vital factor in its educational propaganda and the workers are everywhere being aroused to the necessity of building up a working class press to champion their cause and to discuss current issues from their point of view for the enlightenment of the masses.

This Is Our Year.

Comrades and friends, the campaign before us gives us our supreme opportunity to reach the American people. They have but to know the true meaning of Socialism to accept its philosophy and the true mission of the Socialist party to give it their support. Let us all unite as we never have before to place the issue of Socialism squarely before the masses. For years they have been deceived, misled and betrayed, and they are now hungering for the true gospel of relief and the true message of emancipation.

This is our year in the United States! Socialism is in the very air we breathe. It is the grandest shibboleth that ever inspired men and women to action in this world. In the horizon of labor it shines as a new-risen sun and it is the hope of all humanity.

Onward, comrades, onward in the struggle, until Triumphant Socialism proclaims an Emancipated Race and a New World!

THE FIGHT FOR FREEDOM. Campaign Speech, Pabst Park, Milwaukee, Wis., July 21, 1912.

Friends, Fellow-Socialists and Fellow-Workers: The existing order of things is breaking down. The great forces underlying society are steadily at work. The old order has had its day and all the signs point to an impending change. Society is at once being destroyed and re-created.

The struggle in which we are engaged today is a struggle of economic classes. The supremacy is now held by the capitalist class, who are combined in trusts and control the powers of government. The middle class is struggling desperately to hold its ground against the inroads of its trustified and triumphant competitors.

This war between the great capitalists who are organized in trusts and fortified by the powers of government and the smaller capitalists who constitute the middle class, is one of extermination. The fittest, that is to say the most powerful, will survive. This war gives rise to a variety of issues of which the tariff is the principal one, and these issues are defined in the platforms of the Republican and Democratic parties.

With this war between capitalists for supremacy in their own class and the issues arising from it, the working class have nothing to do, and if they are foolish enough to allow themselves to be drawn into these battles of their masters, as they have so often done in the past, they must continue to suffer the consequences of their folly.

Parties Express Economic Interests.

Let us clearly recognize the forces that are undermining both of the old capitalist parties, creating a new issue, and driving the working class into a party of their own to do battle with their oppressors in the struggle for existence.

Parties but express in political terms the economic interests of those who compose them. This is the rule. The Republican party represents the capitalist class, the Democratic party the middle class and the Socialist party

100

the working class.

There is no fundamental difference between the Republican and Democratic parties. Their principles are identical. They are both capitalist parties and both stand for the capitalist system, and such differences as there are between them involve no principle but are the outgrowth of the conflicting interests of large and small capitalists.

The Republican and Democratic parties are alike threatened with destruction. Their day of usefulness is past and they among them who see the handwriting on the wall and call themselves "Progressives" and "Insurgents," are struggling in vain to adjust these old parties to the new conditions.

Two Economic Classes.

Broadly speaking, there are but two economic classes and the ultimate struggle will narrow down to two political parties. To the extent that the workers unite in their own party, the Socialist party, the capitalists, large and small, are driven into one and the same party. This has happened already in a number of local instances, notably in the City of Milwaukee. Here there is no longer a Republican or Democratic party. These have merged in the same party and it is a capitalist party, by whatever name it may be known.

Temporarily this united capitalist party, composed of the two old ones, may stem the tide of Socialist advance, but nothing more clearly reveals the capitalist class character of the Republican and Democratic parties to their own undoing and the undoing of the capitalist system they represent.

The great capitalists are all conservatives, "standpatters"; they have a strangle-hold upon the situation with no intention of relaxing their grip. Taft and Roosevelt are their candidates. It may be objected that Roosevelt is a "Progressive." That is sheer buncombe. Roosevelt was president almost eight years and his record is known. When he was in office and had the power, he did none of the things, nor attempted to do any of the things he is now talking about so wildly. On the contrary, a more servile functionary to the trusts than Theodore Roosevelt never sat in the presidential chair.

La Follette vs. Roosevelt.

Senator La Follette now makes substantially this same charge against Roosevelt, but by some strange oversight the senator did not discover that Roosevelt's presidential record was a trust record until after Roosevelt threw him down in the "Progressive" scramble for the Republican nomination.

When Senator La Follette supposed he had Roosevelt's backing, he pronounced him "the greatest man in the world," and it was only after he fell victim to Roosevelt's duplicity that he made the discovery that Roosevelt had always been the tool of the trusts and the enemy of the people.

Test of Parties.

There is one infallible test that fixes the status of a political party and its candidates. Who finances them?

With this test applied to Theodore Roosevelt we have no trouble in locating him. He is above all "a practical man." He was practical in allowing the steel trust to raid the Tennessee Coal and Iron Company; he was practical when he legalized the notorious "Alton Steal"; he was practical when he had Harriman raise $240,000 for his campaign fund, and he is practical now in having the steel trust and the harvester trust, who made an anteroom of the White House when he was president, pour out their slush funds by millions to put him back in the White House and keep him there.

Financed by the Trusts.

Taft and Roosevelt, and the Republican party of which they are the candidates, are all financed by the trusts, and is it necessary to add that the trusts also consist of practical men and that they do not finance a candidate or a party they do not control?

Is the man not foolish, to the verge of being feeble-minded, who imagines that great trust magnates, such as Perkins, McCormick and Munsey, are flooding the country with Roosevelt money because he is the champion of progressive principles and the friend of the common people?

The truth is that if the Bull Moose candidate dared to permit an itemized publication of his campaign contributions in his present mad and disgraceful pursuit of the presidency, as he has been so often challenged to do by Senator La Follette, it would paralyze him and scandalize the nation.

Roosevelt must stand upon the record he made when he was president and had the power, and not upon his empty promises as a ranting demagogue and a vote-seeking politician.

For the very reason that the trusts are pouring out their millions to literally buy his nomination and election and force him into the White House for a third term, and if possible for life, the people should rise in their might and repudiate him as they never have repudiated a recreant official who betrayed his trust.

So much for the Republican party, led by Lincoln half a century ago as the party of the people in the struggle for the overthrow of chattel slavery, and now being scuttled by Taft and Roosevelt in base servility to the plutocracy.

The Democratic Party.

The Democratic party, like its Republican ally, is a capitalist party, the only difference being that it represents the minor divisions of the capitalist class. It is true that there are some plutocrats and trust magnates in the Democratic party, but as a rule it is composed of the smaller capitalists who have been worsted by the larger ones and are now demanding that the trusts be destroyed and, in effect, that the laws of industrial evolution be suspended.

The Democratic party, like the Republican party, is financed by the capitalist class. Belmont, Ryan, Roger Sullivan, Taggart and Hinky Dink are liberal contributors to its fund. The Tammany organization in New York, notorious for its corruption and for its subserviency to the powers that rule in capitalist society, is one of the controlling factors in the Democratic party.

Woodrow Wilson is the candidate of the Democratic party for president. He was seized upon as a "progressive"; as a man who would appeal to the common people, but he never could have been nominated without the votes controlled by Tammany and the "predatory interests" so fiercely denounced in the convention by William Jennings Bryan.

It is true that Woodrow Wilson was not the first choice of Belmont,

103

Ryan, Murphy and the Tammany corruptionists, but he was nevertheless satisfactory to them or they would not have agreed to his nomination, and since the convention it is quite apparent that Wilson has a working agreement and a perfect understanding with the predatory interests which Bryan sought to scourge from the convention.

Bryan and Wilson.

In his speech before the delegates denouncing Ryan, Belmont and Murphy, Bryan solemnly declared that no candidate receiving their votes and the votes of Murphy's "ninety wax figures" could have his support. Woodrow Wilson received these votes and without these and other votes controlled by "the interests" he could not have been nominated, and if Bryan now supports him he simply stultifies himself before the American people.

Mr. Wilson is no more the candidate of the working class than is Mr. Taft or Mr. Roosevelt. Neither one of them has ever been identified with the working class, has ever associated with the working class, except when their votes were wanted, or would dare to avow himself the candidate of the working class.

When the recent strikes occurred at Perth Amboy and other industrial centers in New Jersey, Governor Woodrow Wilson ordered the militia out to shoot down the strikers just as Governor Theodore Roosevelt ordered out the soldiers to murder the strikers at Croton Dam, N. Y., for demanding the enforcement of the state laws against the contractors.

They Reek With Corruption.

Both the Republican and Democratic parties reek with corruption in their servility to the capitalist class, and both are torn with strife in their mad scramble for the spoils of office.

The Democratic party has had little excuse for existence since the Civil War, and its utter impotency to deal with present conditions was made glaringly manifest during its brief lease of power under the Cleveland administration. Should this party succeed to national power once more, seething as it is with conflicting elements which are held together by the prospect of official spoils, its career as a national party would be brought to an early close by self-destruction.

The Republican convention at Chicago and the Democratic convention at Baltimore were composed of professional politicians, office-holders, office-seekers, capitalists, retainers, and swarms of parasites and mercenaries of all descriptions.

There were no workingmen in either convention. They were not fit to be there. All they are fit for is to march in the mud, yell themselves hoarse, and ratify the choice of their masters on election day.

The working class was not represented in the Republican convention at Chicago or the Democratic convention at Baltimore. Those were the political conventions of the capitalist class and the few flattering platform phrases in reference to labor were incorporated for the sole purpose of catching the votes of the working class.

Let the American workers remember that they are not fit to sit as delegates in a Republican or Democratic national convention; that they are not fit to write a Republican or Democratic national platform; that all they are fit for is to elect the candidates of their masters to office so that when they go out on strike against starvation they may be shot dead in their tracks as the reward of their servility to their masters and their treason to themselves.

Vital Issue Ignored.

The vital issue before the country and the world is not touched, nor even mentioned in the Republican or Democratic platforms. Wage-slavery under capitalism, the legalized robbery of the workers of what is produced by their labor, is the fundamental crime against modern humanity, but there is no room for the mention of this vital fact, this living issue in the platforms of the Republican and Democratic parties. They continue to babble about the tariff and other inconsequential matters to obscure the real issue and wheedle the workers into voting them into power once more.

These parties have been in power all these years, why have they not settled the tariff and the currency and such other matters as make up their platform pledges?

Let Them Act Now.

While the Republican convention was in session at Chicago and while the Democratic convention was in session at Baltimore, the Republican and Democratic congress was also in session at Washington. These parties already have the power to make good their promises, then why do they not exercise that power to redeem their pledges and afford relief to the people?

In other words, why do not the Republican and Democratic parties perform at Washington instead of promising at Chicago and Baltimore? How many more years of power do they require to demonstrate that they are the parties of the capitalist class and that they never intend to legislate in the interest of the working class, or provide relief for the suffering people.

The Republican and Democratic platforms are filled with empty platitudes and meaningless phrases, but they are discreetly silent about the millions of unemployed, about the starvation wages of factory slaves, about the women and children who are crushed, debased and slowly tortured to death by the moloch of capitalism, about the white slave traffic, about the bitter poverty of the masses and their hopeless future, and about every other vital question which is worthy of an instant's consideration by any intelligent human being.

The Socialist Party.

In contrast with these impotent, corrupt and senile capitalist parties, without principles and without ideals, stands the virile young working class party, the international Socialist party of the world. The convention which nominated its candidates and wrote its platform at Indianapolis was a working class convention.

The Socialist party is the only party which honestly represents the working class in this campaign and the only party that has a moral right to appeal to the allegiance and support of the workers and producers of the nation.

I am not asking you to give your votes to this party but only that you read its platform, study its program, and satisfy yourselves as to what its principles are, what it stands for, and what it expects to accomplish.

The Socialist party being the political expression of the rising working class stands for the absolute overthrow of the existing capitalist system and for the reorganization of society into an industrial and social democracy.

Death to Wage-Slavery.

This will mean an end to the private ownership of the means of life; it will mean an end to wage-slavery; it will mean an end to the army of the unemployed; it will mean an end to the poverty of the masses, the prostitution of womanhood, and the murder of childhood.

It will mean the beginning of a new era of civilization; the dawn of a happier day for the children of men. It will mean that this earth is for those who inhabit it and wealth for those who produce it. If will mean society organized upon a co-operative basis, collectively owning the sources of wealth and the means of production, and producing wealth to satisfy human wants and not to gorge a privileged few. It will mean that there shall be work for the workers and that all shall be workers, and it will also mean that there shall be leisure for the workers and that all shall enjoy it. It will mean that women shall be the comrades and equals of men, sharing with them on equal terms the opportunities as well as the responsibilities, the benefits as well as the burdens of civilized life.

The Socialist party, the first and only international party, is rising grandly to power all around the world. In every land beneath the sun it is the party of the dispossessed, the impoverished and the heavy-laden.

It is the twentieth century party of human emancipation.

It stands for a world-wide democracy, for the freedom of every man, woman and child, and for the civilization of all mankind.

The Socialist party buys no votes. It scorns to traffic in ignorance. It realizes that education, knowledge and the powers these confer are the only means of achieving a decided and permanent victory for the people.

A Clean Campaign.

The campaign of the Socialist party is a clean campaign; it is essentially educational; an appeal to intelligence, to manliness, to womanliness, and to all things of good report.

The workers are opening their eyes at last. They are beginning to see the light. They are taking heart of hope because they are becoming conscious of their power.

They are rallying to the standard of the Socialist party because they know that this is their party and that here they are master, and here they sit at their own political hearthstone and fireside.

No longer can the workers be pitted against each other in capitalist parties by designing politicians to their mutual undoing. They have made the discovery that they have brains as well as hands, that they can think as well as work, and that they do not need politicians to advise them how to vote, nor masters to rob them of the fruits of their labor.

Slowly but surely there is being established the economic and political unity and solidarity of the workers of the world. The Socialist party is the political expression of that unity and solidarity.

Unity the Keynote.

I appeal to the workers assembled here today in the name of the Socialist party. I appeal to you as one of you to unite and make common cause in this great struggle.

To the extent that you have made progress, to the extent that you have developed power, and to the extent that you have achieved victory, to that extent you are indebted to your own class-conscious efforts and your own industrial and political organization. To the extent that you lack power, to the extent that you are defeated and kept in bondage, to that extent you lack in economic and political solidarity.

Rightly organized and soundly disciplined on both the economic and political fields, the working class can prevail against the world.

The economic organization and the political party of the working class must both be revolutionary and they must work together hand in hand.

Industrial unionism means industrial solidarity, but craft unionism means division and disaster. The printing trades pitted against each other in Chicago in their struggle with the newspaper trust furnish a fatal illustration of the weakness and treachery of craft division in the present industrial conflict.

The Workers of Milwaukee.

The workers of Milwaukee have to an exceptional extent overcome the obstacles to unity and have worked together with signal success on both the economic and political fields. I appeal to them in the name of the future to get closer and closer together in the bonds of economic and political solidarity. If they do this their complete and final victory is assured.

The Socialist party of Milwaukee has marched steadily to the front since it first began its career. Its latest defeat was its greatest victory. It forced the Republicans and Democrats to unmask and to fly into each other's arms. There is no Republican or Democratic party in Milwaukee. They are dead, and in the coming election their remains, masquerading as a party of the people, will be buried by the Socialist party.

The First Congressman.

The Socialists of Milwaukee will always have the distinction of having elected the first representative of the working class to the congress of the United States. Victor L. Berger has made good at Washington. For the first time since he is a member the voice of labor has been distinctly heard on the floors of congress, and in every emergency when the working class needed a champion at the seat of power, they found him ready and eager to espouse their cause and defend their interests.

It was to defeat Berger's re-election that the Republicans and Democrats in Milwaukee combined, just as they did to defeat Emil Seidel for mayor and drive the Socialist administration from power.

But Berger is making a record at Washington and the Socialist administration made a record in Milwaukee that will stand the test of time, and if the workers now rally their forces in support of Berger, he will be triumphantly re-elected against the combined opposition of the old parties, and in the next municipal election the City of Milwaukee will be permanently restored to a Socialist administration.

Comrades, you are face to face with the greatest struggle you have ever had since the Socialist party was organized. You are now to be tested in every fiber as to your fitness to hold the ground you have gained and to press on to greater victories. May you be permeated to the core with the spirit of the Socialist movement and enter the fray resolved that victory shall be inscribed upon your banners.

Ettor and Giovannitti.

I must not fail in the presence of all these workers to speak of Joseph Ettor and Arturo Giovannitti, the leaders of the Lawrence strike, who are in prison and soon to be tried upon the charge of murder, of which they are as innocent as if they had never been born.

This infamous charge has been trumped up against them by the defeated mill owners for no other reason than that they stood up bravely and fought successfully against great odds, the battles of the wage-slaves of the mills. Unless the workers unite in support of these two leaders they may be sent to the electric chair. Should we suffer these brave comrades to fall victims to such a monstrous crime, it would be a foul and indelible blot upon the whole labor movement. Let us arouse the workers of the nation in their behalf and prove to them when their trial takes place that we are as true to them as they were to the wage-slaves in the industrial battle at Lawrence.

Comrades, this is our year! Let us rise to our full stature, summon our united powers, and strike a blow for freedom that will be felt around the world!

dec
CAPITALISM AND SOCIALISM. Campaign Speech, Lyceum Theatre, Fergus Falls, Minn., August 27, 1912.

Friends and Fellow-Workers: The spirit of our time is revolutionary and growing, more so every day. A new social order is struggling into existence. The old economic foundation of society is breaking up and the social fabric is beginning to totter. The capitalist system is doomed. The signs of change confront us upon every hand.

Social changes are preceded by agitation and unrest among the masses. We are today in the transition period between decaying capitalism and growing Socialism. The old system is being shaken to its foundations by the forces underlying it and its passing is but a question of time. The new system that is to succeed the old is developing within the old and its outline is clearly revealed in its spirit of mutualism and its co-operative manifestations.

For countless ages the world has been a vast battlefield and the struggle for existence a perpetual conflict. Primitive peoples were compelled to fight nature to extort from her the means of livelihood. Since the forces of nature have been conquered and nations have become civilized the struggle of men is no longer to overcome nature but with one another for existence.

In this struggle which has appealed to the basest and not to the best in man the cunning few have triumphed and now have the masses at their mercy. These few are closely allied in, their economic mastery as they are also in their control of the political machinery. Their money and their mercenaries controlled the Republican convention at Chicago, wrote its platform and dictated its nominees, and the same is true of the Democratic convention at Baltimore.

As for the so-called Progressive convention, it is sufficient to say that there is no attempt to conceal the fact that it was financed and controlled by three conspicuous representatives of the plutocracy which largely owns and rules the land.

Political parties are responsive to the interests of those who finance them. This is the infallible test of their character and applied to the Republican, Democratic and Progressive parties, these parties stand forth as the several political expressions of the several divisions of the capitalist class. The funds of all these parties are furnished by the capitalist class for the reason, and only for the reason, that they represent the interests of that class.

Professional politicians of whatever party are very much alike and in one respect at least they are like workingmen, they serve the interests of their masters, and for the same reason.

The patriotism of professional politicians is reflected in the material interests of the master class and this fact has become so apparent that their noisy theatricals have lost their magic and now excite but the scorn and derision of intelligent working men and women.

The Republican, Democratic and Progressive conventions were composed in the main and controlled entirely by professional politicians in the service of the ruling class.

There were no working men and no working women at the Republican convention, the Democratic convention, or the Progressive convention.

These were clearly not working class conventions. Ladies and gentlemen of leisure were in evidence at them all. Wage-slaves would not have been tolerated in their company. They represented the wealth and culture and refinement of society and they were there to applaud and smile approval upon the professional politicians and patriots who were doing their work.

But there was a fourth convention held this year which did not attract the wealthy and leisure classes. It was a convention great in purpose, though not big in numbers. This convention was held at Indianapolis and represented the working class. The delegates who composed this convention were chosen by the workers and paid by the workers to represent the interest of the workers and to clear the way for the workers in the present campaign.

The Socialist convention was the only democratic convention and the only progressive convention held this year; the only convention that represented a dues-paying party membership and whose acts before becoming effective must be ratified by a referendum vote of the party.

112

The Socialist party is the only party in this campaign that stands against the present system and for the rule of the people; the only party that boldly avows itself the party of the working class and its purpose the overthrow of wage-slavery.

So long as the present system of capitalism prevails and the few are allowed to own the nation's industries, the toiling masses will be struggling in the hell of poverty as they are today. To tell them that juggling with the tariff will change this beastly and disgraceful condition is to insult their intelligence. The professional politicians who have been harping upon this string since infant industries have become giant monopolies know better. Their stock in trade is the credulity of the masses.

The exploited wage-slaves of free trade England and of the highly protected United States are the victims of the same capitalism; in England the politicians tell them they are suffering because they have no protective tariff and in the United States they tell them that the tariff is the cause of their poverty.

And this is the kind of a confidence game the professional politicians have been playing with the workers of all nations all these years. To keep them in subjection by playing upon their ignorance is the rule that governs their campaigns for votes among the workers. The "issues" upon which they keep the workers divided into hostile camps are of their own making.

Since the foundation of the government one or the other of these capitalist parties has been in power and under their administration the working and producing millions have been reduced to poverty and slavery. Professor Scott Nearing has shown in his work on the wages of American workers that half of the adult males of the United States are earning less than $500; that three-quarters of them are earning less than $600 a year; that nine-tenths of them are receiving less than $900 a year, while 10 per cent only receive more than that figure.

Professor Nearing also shows the starvation wages for which women are compelled to work in the present system. One-fifth of the whole number of women workers receive less than $200 per year; three-fifths receive less than $325; nine-tenths receive less than $500. Only one-twentieth of the women employed are paid more than $600 per year.

These figures bear out the report of the Chicago vice commission to

113

the effect that the low wages of women and girls go hand in hand with prostitution. Despite all attempts to control the white slave traffic, which is now organized as one of the great profit-extorting trusts, along with the rest of the trusts, prostitution, like a terrible cancer, is eating out the very heart of our civilization.

And in the presence of this appalling condition the professional politicians prattle about tariff revision and indulge in silly twaddle about currency reform and regulation of the trusts.

The Socialist party is absolutely the only party which faces conditions as they are and declares unhesitatingly that it has a definite and concrete plan and program for dealing with these conditions.

The Socialist party as the party of the exploited workers in the mills and mines, on the railways and on the farms, the workers of both sexes and all races and colors, the working class in a word, constituting a great majority of the people and in fact THE PEOPLE, demands that the nation's industries shall be taken over by the nation and that the nation's workers shall operate them for the benefit of the whole people.

Private ownership and competition have had their day. The Socialist party stands for social ownership and co-operation. The one is Capitalism; the other Socialism. The one industrial despotism, the other industrial democracy.

The Republican, Democratic and Progressive parties all stand for private ownership and competition. The Socialist party alone stands for social ownership and co-operation.

The Republican, Democratic and Progressive parties believe in regulating the trusts; the Socialist party believes in owning them, so that all the people may get the benefit of them instead of a few being made plutocrats and the masses impoverished.

The Republican, Democratic and Progressive parties uphold the wage system; the Socialist party demands its overthrow.

It is under the wage system that the 22,000 operatives in the cotton and woolen mills at Lawrence, Massachusetts, have been compelled to work, or slave rather, according to Commissioner Neill, for an average of $8.76 per family. To earn this average wage, according to the commissioner's official report, requires the combined service of father, mother and three children.

This is slavery with a vengeance. The mill is a sweat-hole; the hovel a breeding-pen. Home there is none. And there never will be under the wage system.

What have the Republican, Democratic and Progressive parties to offer to the wage-slaves of Lawrence, to the wage-slaves of the steel trust, to the wage-slaves of the mines, to the wage-slaves of the lumber and turpentine camps of the South, the wage-slaves of the railroads, the millions of them, male and female, black and white and yellow and brown, who produce all this nation's wealth, support its government and conserve its civilization, and without whom industry would be paralyzed and the nation helpless? What, I ask, has any of these capitalist parties, or all of them combined, for the working and producing class in this campaign? Nothing. Absolutely nothing.

These parties are bidding stronger than ever for the labor vote this year. That vote is now not so easily delivered as in the past. The competition for the votes of the wage-workers is the distinguishing feature of the present campaign. Thousands of workers are now doing their own thinking. They have discovered that workers are as much out of place in a capitalist party as capitalists are in a workers' party. They have also found that politics express class interests and that the interests of those who make the wealth and those who take it are not identical. That is where the Socialist party comes in and where the workers come in the Socialist party.

The working class is in politics this year. It has always been in politics for its master; this year it is in politics for itself.

The most promising fact in the world today is the fact that labor is organizing its power; its economic power and its political power.

The workers who have made the world and who support the world, are preparing to take possession of the world. This is the meaning of Socialism and is what the Socialist party stands for in this campaign.

We demand the machinery of production in the name of the workers and the control of society in the name of the people. We demand the abolition of capitalism and wage-slavery and the surrender of the capitalist class. We demand the complete enfranchisement of women and the equal rights of all the people regardless of race, color, creed or nationality. We demand that child labor shall cease once and forever and that all children born into the world shall have equal opportunity to grow up, to be educated,

115

to have healthy bodies and trained minds, and to develop and freely express the best there is in them in mental, moral and physical achievement.

We demand complete control of industry by the workers; we demand all the wealth they produce for their own enjoyment, and we demand the earth for all the people.